One a Day

Vendon Wright

authorHOUSE®

AuthorHouse™ UK Ltd.
1663 Liberty Drive
Bloomington, IN 47403 USA
www.authorhouse.co.uk
Phone: 0800.197.4150

Published by AuthorHouse 07/16/2014

ISBN: 978-1-4969-8630-6 (sc)
ISBN: 978-1-4969-8631-3 (e)

Introduction

We encounter numerous obstacles that challenge us on every level. They vary from stressful situations to issues concerning our perception of ourselves. Some of the challenges put us under so much pressure that there are days where we feel as though we could do with a little help and advice. Since the daily problems change, it is also necessary to have a variety of techniques to counter them.

This book will teach you how to be happier with your life by addressing the main principals in greater detail. It covers techniques on building up your confidence, communication skills, how to handle stress, handling rejection and dealing with criticism. It teaches you how to improve your life step by step until you are strong enough to face all your challenges.

When you feel more positive about yourself it is far easier to become successful as you can handle more pressure. Some days you will need tips on self help and other days you will need advice on becoming more successful.

To live a happier life doesn't always mean to have more money, even though it does help. Sometimes all you need is advice on how to be more assertive in various situations.

This book has an inspirational phrase for every day of the year. Read one a day and watch your personality change for the better at the same time as becoming more confident and successful.

How to use

A   It is recommended that you first read the phrases in their original order as they have been carefully selected to represent your growth in knowledge, confidence and strength as time goes on. Each phrase prepares you for the increasing amount of pressure that you will encounter on the path to enlightenment.

B   Once you have fully digested the information contained in this book it is highly recommended that you refer to it on a regular basis to avoid negativity. This can be done by selecting phrases randomly. Think of a number between one and three hundred and sixty five and then look it up. You must be disciplined to follow that advice throughout the day.

C   You can play a game and have fun with your friends. Ask someone else to select a number. Then you can all use the advice throughout the day.

D   Another way of utilising the information is to create cards with the numbers on. Shuffle the cards and then choose one each day. You will be amazed with the way the cards seem to read your mind as it chooses a phrase that you were in need of.

There is a phrase for every day of the year. Use them wisely to higher your tolerance level. Although it is up to you to decide which method to use, it is not advised to read them all in one session. There is far too much information to process and you will overload your mind with positive thoughts.

Medicine - to help you cope with every situation

1   Have goals and dreams to work towards.

It is important to have things to work towards because it helps to concentrate your mind on something constructive and meaningful. If you haven't got any goals then find some or you will find yourself concentrating on the wrong things in life. It starts with a dream. Is there a career that you want? What kind of job is it? Are you interested in owning your own business? There's no harm with dreaming. Dreamers are achievers so start dreaming.

2   Think positive not negative.

Negative thoughts can grow in our mind until they consume us. They eat away at everything good until we almost forget how to think positively. We are prone to assume that things will go wrong. Allowing negative thoughts to grow holds us back from achieving more. Learn to dismiss them and start to concentrate on positive thoughts. Hidden beneath all that negativity are the thoughts that will help you excel. Fill your mind with positive thoughts and shut out the negative ones. If you really want to get more out of life, think positively.

3   If I think I can, I can.

There are many self help techniques that will help you think better of yourself. They include phrases that you need to use verbally. It's time to start talking positively to yourself. Repeating it will make you feel slightly uncomfortable at first but the more you use it, the easier it gets. It will encourage you to try harder at completing challenges. Use it all day to assist you in various situations. Be brave and try it!

4   I'll feel better tomorrow.

Has it been a difficult day today? Sometimes we wear ourselves out trying to do too much or just thinking too much. Maybe tomorrow you will feel as though you have more strength to carry on where you left off. Frequently tell yourself that you will feel better tomorrow. Then you won't feel like a failure. Concentrate on something more positive for the rest of the day.

5   I'm not scared.

Sometimes we are in two minds whether to proceed with a difficult task. The thought of achieving it excites us but the obstacles before us sends a chill down our spine. A few words of encouragement will persuade you to make the right choice. Repeat this phrase several times and it will point you in the right direction. Your mind will develop more positive thoughts to assist you.

6   Think of happy thoughts.

Happy thoughts can be of something that has happened in the past, something that is happening now or something that you would like to happen in the future. Is there someone that you have feelings for? Imagine if they said 'Yes,' would that make you happy? Is it a job that you are trying to get? Would it make you happy if you got the job? Would you like to go on holiday? Where would you go? Think of different happy thoughts for the whole day.

7   Good things come to those who wait.

Work hard at everything that you desire in life. Be determined to do what ever it takes to succeed. When you have put all the pieces together, then it's only a matter of time before it starts working for you. Be patient, wait and you will see. Good things are about to happen in your life.

8 Some will, some won't.

The idea you have sounds good. People have shown good interest in it but you are looking for a few more people to reach your goal. Unfortunately not everyone will see your idea from the same perspective as you. When you adopt this positive attitude towards life, it helps you in coping with negative responses. Keep looking for more people and learn to ignore the rest.

9 Everyone has problems.

Many of us think that we are the only one with problems. This is because we are so used to seeing the negative side of life that we can't comprehend any other way. We do have problems but so does everybody else. The sooner we realise this, the quicker we can learn to enjoy our lives, despite our problems. If anyone complains today, use this phrase and observe their response.

10 Don't let anyone tell you that you can't.

Some people have a nasty habit of telling us that we can't achieve our goals and dreams. Most of them don't even understand the concept of what we are trying to achieve but they always have plenty to comment on. If they are generally known to discourage people, then don't listen to them. Avoid these people whenever you can to prevent their negative influences from affecting you.

11   Dream build.

Most of us are too scared to dream build just in case we don't achieve our goals. We need to realise that we will achieve more when we dream build more often. Visualise the things that you desire in greater detail. Nobody said that you have to achieve everything that you desire. Dream building is an important ingredient in developing a positive character. Have you been thinking about moving house? Where would it be? How many bedrooms? What kind of furniture would you have? What would your garden be like?

Dream building doesn't have to be of material things. I sometimes dream build about having my eyesight back. I would go for long walks and look at the beautiful flowers all around. See how detailed you can make your dreams.

12   Fear is false.

Fear can grow to a level that we actually think that it's going to happen. We have to be careful not to let fear rule us. Look around you; fear is everywhere yet nowhere. We have fear of being ill yet our doctor has repeatedly told us that there is nothing wrong. We fear people that are taller than us, yet they turn out to be as gentle as a puppy dog. We fear people from other backgrounds, yet they turn out to be our best friend. Fear is: false evidence appearing to be real. It appears to be real from the increased amount of time and effort that we spend on developing our thoughts. It's time to concentrate your thoughts on something else and watch your fears fade away.

13   Enjoy your life.

We all have problems to a certain degree. Some of them are bigger than other people's but we are still expected to find a way to enjoy our lives. We are only here for a short wile so we haven't got time to waste. Be almost in a hurry to enjoy the wonders of the world. The older you are, the less agile you will become. Then it is harder to appreciate the true beauties of the world. Don't let life pass you by. Find more ways to enjoy your life. The true meaning of life is to enjoy your life despite the challenges that you will encounter.

14   I'm a winner.

Self help is a necessary input required in order to reach success. We need to realise that we are not worthless and that we will become successful once we begin to believe in ourselves. Use this phrase verbally to enhance its power. Express each word with great emphasis. When you keep repeating that you are a winner, eventually you will believe that you are a winner.

15   Be a great listener.

Are you an attention seeker that prefers to talk a lot? Have you ever come away from a conversation and wondered what the other person had to say? That's because you did all the talking! You never gave them a chance to speak much. Start listening to other people. It is important to teach yourself how to think about other people. Next time a friend calls you for help, just listen to them. Don't even offer your opinion. Sometimes people want you to help them by just listening to their dissatisfactions. God gave us two ears and one mouth! That means that we should listen to people twice as much as we speak.

16   Appreciate what you can do.

Are you lazy? I hope not! Many of us take life for granted and don't appreciate the things that we can do until it's too late. A simple task like walking; many of us prefer to drive but when we lose a leg we then wish that we had it back so that we could be able to walk again. When was the last time you went for a walk? When was the last time you read a book and I mean before reading this one? Perform simple tasks while you can.

17   Everyone has choices.

Some people consistently make the wrong choices in life and then complain that life doesn't like them. Do you have friends similar to that too? It's time to stop blaming other people for your wrong choices and start to make better ones. We always have two choices. Each choice we make is similar to taking another step forward in life. Each step we take leads us to two more choices. When you make a wrong choice, you still reach the next step where you can admit defeat or learn from it. Next time you take a step, tread carefully.

18   When you're feeling down, go up.

Everyone feels down at some stage in their lives, so you are not alone when you feel as though your world has fallen apart. It's at times like this when we need to turn to more positive people to help motivate us back on our feet. The only problem is that sometimes positive people make us feel more useless and hopeless so we prefer to stay away from them. It's time you realise that it is those same positive people that you will need to pick you back up. If you turn to a doctor or a counsellor for advice, it is always positive information that they feed you. They never tell you to stay down... do they? The sooner you realise this, the faster you will return to reality.

19   Make a decision.

Are you unsure with what to do? Many of us are indecisive and spend too much time considering all the possibilities to simple issues. When we go out to dinner, we regularly prefer other people to select which meal to eat off the menu before we make a decision. The problem with this is that they too are expecting you to be the first to decide. If you have been thinking about something for a while, then today you have to make a decision either way.

20   Never, never give up.

Did things not work out? At least you tried. Make your goals and dreams important to you. Now make another decision, never to give up trying. We all feel like giving up on something that's worth pursuing. As long as you never actually give up, there's always another chance to succeed. The longer you stay in the race, the more chances of success.

21   Workers are achievers.

When you work hard enough, you will achieve more. Look around at most of the people that achieve more, they are still working when others are sat around watching television. If you really want more out of life then start by watching television less. Be prepared to work extra hard for what you desire.

22   Life is tremendous.

I hope that made you laugh! If it didn't, say it again: life is tremendous! At this stage in your life it might not feel tremendous but it is an attitude you are going to have to adopt so that you see a different side to life. When someone asks you how you feel say 'I feel tremendous' now watch them laugh or at least smile.

23   I haven't got any problems.

It really does seem as though we have some serious problems and issues to overcome. The feelings we are experiencing within us has multiplied in conjunction with the amount of passion we have attached to them. Compared to some people, our problems are quite small. We overcome problems faster when we believe that we haven't got any. Our ability to deal with problems will increase as our problems fade away.

24   Smile.

When was the last time that you smiled? Some of us are so busy trying to sort out the various problems in our lives that we don't leave enough time to smile. Our smile is replaced with a frown everytime we concentrate on a problem. When we force ourselves to smile more, it magically helps us in coping with our problems. Force yourself to walk around with a smile on your face. I'm sure that you look like a completely different person! Find something to smile about. Let your personality radiate through your smile. Remind yourself on a regular basis to smile. We should aim to smile at least once a day.

25   I feel great.

Keep telling yourself that you feel great and you will become a happier person. The next time someone asks you how you are, don't answer with 'fine'. This phrase is far too common. It means that you do have a problem and that you are probably going to share it with them. Next time someone asks you how you are, answer with 'I feel great'. Now watch their response. Add some spice to your life and have some fun with observing the different responses that you will receive. Soon other people will want some of your positive attitude.

26   Next.

We are presented with problems on a daily basis, some of which seem to have no clear solution. Although we have built up our strength to cope with them, it also appears that we are wasting too much time and effort on overcoming them. Are you ready for the next one? Believe that you will overcome the problem and that you are ready for the next one. Suppose you are only going to encounter ten major problems in life and then you will find peace and happiness, would you welcome your next problem to hastily get to your last? Well it's true. You have to get through a series of difficult problems before you will find happiness and success. Don't waste any more time. Move onto your next challenge.

27   Think big.

Most of us are scared of thinking big just in case we don't achieve our dreams. Thinking big helps to become more ambitious. It also encourages us to think more positively. There are no guarantees but you stand a better chance of achieving more by first perceiving it. Most inventions would have remained dormant if everyone was afraid to visualise their ideas. Stretch your mind to a new limit. Amplify those thoughts that you have suppressed to avoid heartache and pain.

28   Have fun.

Do you take life too seriously? Well don't! We have all worked hard to get where we are in life. The obstacles that we encounter have forced us to devote more time than we prefer in overcoming them. Try not to be so serious about everything. Leave some space in your life to have some fun. Go and do something wild! Let your hair down and have some more fun. The more fun you have, the less stressed you will feel. It will encourage you to approach challenges from a different angle. Too much work and not enough play is not good for your health. Do something that makes you smile or even laugh. Have more fun and you will become unbelievably happy.

29 Go for it.

Do you want more out of life? You should have had enough fun now, so it's time to get back to work. The happier you feel, the more challenges you will be prepared to take on. Have you been thinking of going back to college? Have you been thinking of a career change? Set your eyes on a goal and... go for it.

30 Be an encourager.

It has probably been several weeks since you last put other people first. Thinking of other people shows that you are a kind hearted person. Today you have to take your eyes off yourself and encourage someone else to think more positively about themself.

31 It's okay to cry.

Sometimes things don't work out as planned. After putting sufficient effort into a challenge, things go wrong. Maybe someone has put you down despite all your efforts, or maybe you received some bad news. You are allowed to cry. Expressing your feelings is an excellent way of getting something off your chest. It lightens the load so that your body is under less pressure.

32 Leaders lead.

Have you been considering acting on an idea for a while? Would you prefer someone else to try it first? Why? Don't wait for other people to take the lead. Just because something works for someone else, it doesn't mean that it will work for you. When you want something to work, you have to be prepared to work for it. It's time for you to try things first and not wait to see if it works for someone else.

33   I feel wonderful.

Encourage yourself by believing you are capable of many things. This is another positive phrase to use when people ask you how you are feeling. It will cheer other people up hearing your positive response. Utilize positive phrases as they will build your self confidence.

34   Stop moaning.

Be careful not to moan too much. Moaning can drain away your positive energy causing your personality to dramatically change. You do have problems but so does everyone else. Why moan to other people about your problems? They will be more interested in sorting out their own. Set yourself some tasks to add a little more fun to your life. You are not allowed to moan today! That's right; today is a moan free day. See how long you can last without moaning.

35   I'm gorgeous.

Are you? It seems that you still don't think very highly of yourself. You are gorgeous. Now you need to believe that you are. The more highly you think of yourself the more confident you will feel. Change the distorted mirror that you keep looking through for a clearer one. If you still don't believe that you are gorgeous, listen to your friends that are saying that you are.

36   I am blessed.

Sometimes I think of my own problems and wonder why I am disabled and why I am suffering so much. Have you had similar thoughts? After that thought, I turn my attention on some other people's problems to see what I can learn. I have seen people that have not been able to leave hospital for weeks. I have also seen people that are paralysed or people that only have a few months to live. It's at times like this that I realise that I am blessed. Maybe it's time you realised that you are blessed too.

37   You can do it.

As you practice the different quotes, your confidence should be growing too. They encourage you to deal with situations more positively. Speak to yourself more frequently and you will see an even greater difference to your self esteem. When you feel under too much pressure to quit, use this phrase.

38   It will be worth it.

Are you still in two minds whether to go for it or not? Imagine what life would be like if things went according to your plan. Does it feel satisfying? Imagine that you have already achieved your goal. Visualise the benefits and see how excited it makes you become. You should be able to feel the true emotions that will be present when you finally win.

39   Write things down.

Writing things down is another way of remembering important information. Sometimes our mind works overtime and has too much information to process. Then we become confused and then forget things. I'm sure that you don't forget on purpose! Write things down and then you will have a visual backup to refer to at a later date. Writing down your goals in life is also a great idea as it encourages you to work towards them.

40   Do the things people won't do, to have what they can't have.

Many of us want more out of life but we are not prepared to work that little bit harder to achieve them. If we do what the average person does, then we will have what the average person has. Is that what you want? Some people won't do overtime at work because it clashes with their favourite television programme, yet they complain of not having enough money. How can watching television help you get out of debt? Watch less television and do more work.

41   Treat yourself.

I bet you have been waiting for me to say that for ages! You have been working extremely hard for a month and now it's time for a little treat. It is important to treat yourself – not too often though! Too much work and not enough play isn't good for you. Treating yourself is a way of saying 'well done' for all your hard work. Buy yourself a small gift, nothing too extravagant. Go out for lunch or do something fun! Pamper yourself today but it's back to work tomorrow.

42   Believe in yourself.

Have you been doing positive things that you would not have done in the past? Other people knew that you could do it. Now it's time to believe in yourself. Convince yourself even if you start out pretending to believe in yourself. Eventually you will become that person for real.

43   Read happy stories.

There are plenty of happy stories out there to read about. They help bring back a smile to your face. Stories of how people got through difficult moments of their lives will help motivate you to do more with your life. Reading them will make you realise that there is more to life than just moaning about your problems.

44   Have good people skills.

Learn how to deal with people. Find out what people want. Listen to them carefully. Be aware of your body language so that you don't appear to be aggressive. If you are having a dispute with a friend, put your hands down by your side so that it doesn't look as though you want a confrontation – you wouldn't hit your friend... would you?

45   Learn to handle rejection.

Rejection is one of the hardest things to live with. When you can learn to handle rejection, you will be able to handle anything. Believe in yourself. There is nothing wrong with you or any product that you are trying to promote. It is them that are making a big mistake. Find something or someone else to concentrate on. When one door closes another door opens. (Go to number 26)

46   I'm confident.

When you can handle rejection then you really will be confident. Keep telling yourself that you are confident and watch your confidence rapidly grow. It is an excellent phrase to use just before you perform a difficult task. It will help you to approach challenges more positively.

47   Stop waiting until tomorrow.

Why are you waiting until tomorrow? Some of us put tasks off until another day because we can't quite fit it in today. Also some people prefer to leave them until tomorrow as they may cause us too much distress. We need to realise that we can do it now if we had a more positive approach. For some people tomorrow is too late. For others, tomorrow never comes. Do what you need to do... today!

48   Don't cry over spilt milk.

Find a tissue and wipe it up! There are certain things that are worth crying over, like the death of someone close to our heart or over a child that has been seriously hurt. Most of the issues we cry over are not worth the tears. They are simple problems that can be corrected at a later date. Don't cry, do something to improve the situation.

49   You never know what you had until you lose it.

Some of us are not happy with what we have. We constantly try to change things to make them perfect. Sometimes there is nothing wrong with it in the first place. Unfortunately we don't find that out until we have lost it. When it's gone we wish that we had it back, just the way it was. So why are you complaining? Stop trying to make everything perfect. Accept people for who they are and not who you want them to be. Some of you can't be bothered to visit your parents. You treat them as though they are going to be there forever. If you lose them you will wish that you had found more time to visit them when they were alive, so why not do so now?

50   I deserve success.

I believe that you do because: you have worked extra hard; you have learnt to handle rejection; you have put up with a great deal of negative comments; you are a positive thinking person and you have overcome a multitude of problems and challenges. Have you really? Then you deserve to be successful. Say it and don't forget it.

51   Think of something funny.

We all have thoughts that are funny. It could be something that happened to us, something that happened to someone else or something that would be funny if it happened. Reach deep into your minds. There must be something out there that you find funny! Think of something funny today.

52   Don't hold a grudge.

Bottling up all that anger and rage can make you ill. People put too much negative thoughts into issues that are not that important. The anger builds up inside and squeezes out your positive thoughts and you end up feeling ill. The stress of these negative thoughts can lead to anxiety attacks and other medical disorders. Concentrate your thoughts on more important issues. Brush aside the less important ones.

53   It's not over yet.

When something doesn't quite go as planned, it is very tempting to call it a day. Don't give up so easily. Have a positive attitude in these circumstances. Keep telling yourself that it's not over yet. It is another positive way of looking at the challenges that you are experiencing.

54   Calm down.

Easier said than done! Do you rush around frantically? You can't do a hundred things all at the same time – unless you are a woman! Rushing around trying to multitask can agitate you and cause your heart rate to race, which can lead to high blood pressure. Calm down before you do yourself an injury. Try not to think so much. Find some time to relax and then continue what you were doing a little later. You make more mistakes when you are rushing around so slow down.

55   I am ambitious.

Telling yourself that you are ambitious helps you become more business minded. Being ambitious doesn't mean that you have to try every business idea that comes along. It's great to be an entrepreneur but be cautious. Exercise your mind in other positive ways and your confidence in yourself will rapidly grow.

56   I believe in you.

When was the last time that you used that phrase on someone? I believe in you, but you need to believe in other people. Build up other people's confidence by helping them feel more worthy. It's not all about you! There are people out there that need your positive attitude to inspire them. See how many people you can say 'I believe in you' to today.

57   You only have one life.

So why are you wasting it? Some of us spend most of our lives moaning about issues that don't even concern us. We don't find enough time to enjoy what we have. What have you always wanted to do? Is there a country that you have always dreamed of visiting? Why wait until you are too old to enjoy it? Get out and have some fun!

58   Don't worry, be happy.

Haven't you been on holiday again this year? Can't you afford a car? Are you in debt? Don't worry, be happy! Things could be worse. You still have your health. Don't moan about trivial things. A car is a luxury and not a necessity. Most of our worries are about materialistic things that we can do without. There are more important things to worry about. Life could be better but it also could be worse.

59   Create a habit.

You have been taught a variety of techniques to help you think more positively. Now you need to live by them and use them everyday of your life. The principals will change your life for the better. It can be far too easy to forget them and return to a more negative approach to life so constantly think of ways to improve yourself. Think more highly of yourself. Be a good friend and remember to enjoy your life!

60   It's never too late.

Have you given up on someone? Do you think that it's too late to make things work? If they haven't died then it's not too late to make improvements. Maybe you haven't spoken to a family member for years but deep down you would have wanted things to have worked out differently. Do you think that you are too old to return to college? Have you been in the same job for more than thirty years and feel too old to change your career? It's never too late!

61   I'm assertive.

You are today! Put together what you have learnt so far. Be observant of other people's actions. Think ahead so that you are ready with a response. If you can anticipate what people are going to say or do then it helps to make you appear more assertive.

62   If it's to be, it's up to me.

I use this phrase far too many times. I am registered blind and have to rely on other people to help me get around efficiently. Sometimes when I am desperate for help, it isn't convenient for anyone to assist me. It's at times like this when I use it the most and end up doing things myself. You can too. Ask other people for help and assistance whenever necessary. When it is important and they are not available, be prepared to do it yourself.

63   Be passionate.

Many of us want more out of life. Sometimes the only reason we fail to achieve them is due to a lack of passion towards them. Put some emotion and excitement into what you are working on. Do things as though you want to and not like you have to. The more passionate you are, the more time and effort you will invest into acquiring them. Strengthen your passion.

64   Try, try and try again.

We all try things but if we fail most of us give up. If you are serious about something, if you are passionate, you will try again. If you fail again, try again... and again. Thomas Edison invented the light bulb but had over nine hundred failed attempts before he found one that worked. Are you that dedicated to your goals?

65   If the dream is big enough the facts don't count.

What's your dream? We all have dreams, some bigger than others. The bigger dreams are usually the ones that we achieve. This is because we have thought about them more regularly. We then become excited about them and soon feel as though it is important for us to reach them. Our mind then begins to find ways of achieving them despite the obstacles we come across. Don't be scared of dreaming. Make an emotional attachment to them and you will find ways to work towards them.

66   Yes I can.

We can all reach a point where we feel as though we can't go any further. Sometimes we are very tempted to give up. It is a battle to decide whether we should call it a day or try one more time. The more positive you are, the more likely you will continue. Positive phrases help to build up your belief in your abilities. Next time you feel as though you can't proceed, shout 'YES I CAN'.

67   I enjoy a challenge.

Look at problems as challenges. There are many different types of challenges to experience during our lives. Some of them will involve getting very serious about and others can be viewed as a way of keeping us busy. Dealing with some of them can be seen as fun as long as we don't become too serious about the result. When we finally overcome a challenge, it gives us a great sense of achievement. Challenges can either make you or break you – the choice is yours!

68   Music makes me happy.

Music creates a variety of moods that result in us feeling happy or sad. There are tracks that bring back fond memories which lead to us feeling very emotional. Faster tracks tend to make us feel more hyper active. They are used during aerobic classes to encourage us to work harder. Slower music calms us down and helps us to relax at night, especially when we are struggling to sleep. Listening to music takes our mind off a problem and can also drown out a negative thought. Next time you feel overwhelmed with stress, listen to some of your favourite tracks.

69   I have the ability to succeed.

This is probably the most important ingredient in order to succeed. It is the characteristic that deters us from attempting to achieve more. We are capable of more than we realise but we need to believe it in order to speed up the process of success. Use as many self help quotes as possible to enhance your belief in yourself. People have already told you that they believe that you can succeed. It's time you believed it too.

70   Think, before you act.

Have you ever given your opinion and then later on wished that you had handled the situation differently? We sometimes voice our opinion too quickly without considering the after effects of our decision. It then creates more problems than we had in the first place. Think about the benefits of your actions. Will it be worth it? Think about the consequences. Are you sure that it's worth the risk? Stop and think before you act.

71   Speculate to accumulate.

Profitable business ventures cost money. Many of us have great ideas but are not prepared to invest any money into getting them started. Then we wonder why situations fail to materialise. We need to realise that we don't get something for nothing. Owning a well known franchise is far from cheap but worth the money in the end. Be prepared to invest.

72   You can't be up all the time.

When you are feeling down, remember that you are not alone. Not even the most motivated motivator can honestly say that they are always up. The death of someone close always gives you a moment of sadness. Try not to stay down for too long because your negative thoughts can easily multiply out of control.

73   Be thankful for what you have.

You are considered as normal for wanting more out of life. There's no real harm from wanting more as long as it isn't at someone else's expense. Don't give up on ventures that are worth pursuing but be thankful for what you already have. Be thankful for the food you eat because there are many starving children around the world that would feast on the food that you waste without thought. Be thankful for the clothes on your back as there are many people much poorer than yourself. Be thankful for where you live, for there are others who have no roof over their heads. Be thankful for your state of health as there are many people that cannot get around without an assistant. I'm sure that there are other people that envy you so be thankful.

74   I feel lucky.

Have you noticed that you seem to be having more luck? When you feel more positive about yourself you will automatically attempt to accomplish more tasks. This helps to higher your success rate so that you appear to be achieving more. Quote this phrase regularly and watch how luck attaches itself to you. When luck comes knocking at your door, open it and be ready or you might miss your chance of success.

75   Strive for perfection.

A basketball player can start off as a mediocre player. They can be someone who misses most of their attempts to throw the ball into the net. Despite their failed attempts, they are determined to become a successful player. With a positive attitude towards their goal, they can go under an intense course to improve their skills. This will include a countless amount of attempts at throwing the basketball directly into the net. It can take months or even years before their skills are improved to a standard that their coach is happy with. There will be times where they are tempted to quit because of the high volume of challenges they are experiencing but their attempts will vastly improve with time. A skill that started off as your weakness can become your best asset and something that you are renowned for.

76   Be nice to people on the way up, you may need them on the way down.

Life isn't about how much money you can make. You need to have a shining personality or it will be lonely at the top. If the time ever came where you lost your success, who would care? This is why we have been spending so much time building up your character. People care more for people that care about other people.

77   Practice what you preach.

Some people are brilliant at giving advice. When you take a look at their lives you find out that they have similar problems and are doing the opposite to what they are advising you to do. Have you got friends like that... too? Maybe they should take some of the same advice they are sharing. Next time you are giving advice, be prepared to follow it yourself.

78   Observe people's body language.

Have you got any friends that appear to be psychic? They might be psychic but it's much more likely that they are very good at observing people's body language. You can learn to be more perceptive too. Be aware of how people look, talk, stand or sit. If they cross their legs towards you or seem to lean towards you, they are probably interested in what you are saying. People are generally not interested when they have their hands on their hips, arms crossed, hand under chin or are regularly looking away. You can also use body language to determine different moods. If someone is very talkative but one day they are not, they are probably stressed. If someone's shy but is then talking too much, then they are probably... drunk or nervous. Watch people more closely from now on.

79   Be enthusiastic.

Show people that you are interested by expressing yourself more. Raise the tone of your voice in places to show your enthusiasm. Speak faster as though you are in a hurry to get all your words out. Move around more and act excited about every word you are expressing. Put as much effort as possible into everything that you do.

80   You're allowed to make mistakes.

Everyone makes mistakes at some stage of their lives. Some of us are far too hard on ourselves. We punish ourselves for every mistake we make. Give yourself a second chance. Most mistakes can be corrected at a later stage. Find ways to improve your success rate. Take time to work out where you are going wrong. It might turn out that you only needed a slight readjustment to your ideas.

81   I'm not shy.

Being shy is a state of mind. It can be altered by changing the way we think about ourselves. Having this altered view will help us become more confident. The more confident we feel, the more situations we will be able to handle. Repeating it to yourself will lead to you feeling less uncomfortable around other people. Then you will be ready to take on the world. (Go to number 29)

82   Always look on the bright side of life.

The majority of us concentrate on the negative problems that are happening all around us. Everyday we are consistently bombarded with devastating news through the television, newspapers and on the radio. There are many amazing stories of people overcoming huge traumas, yet we hardly get to hear about them. Some of us wish for the weather to be better, yet when it improves we still find something else to complain about. Learn to redirect your thoughts and you will see a different side to life.

83   The hardest step is the first one.

So hurry up and take it! Many of us have interesting ideas but are afraid to make the first move. The fear of failure prevents us from starting on our journey towards success. Just take it. Once you have persuaded yourself to take that all important first step the rest will become easier. Convince yourself to progress forwards or you could always ask a friend to push you on to it. It all starts from that first step.

84   Be prepared to compromise.

It's not easy to compromise because... you're always right! The whole world doesn't need to know that you are right. As long as you know, that's all that matters. Sometimes it's extremely difficult to get other people to see situations from your perspective. If you continue it can lead to frustration so agree to try a different approach.

85   Have faith.

When we encounter a difficult situation, some of us lose faith far too quickly. Learn to pursue important goals. If you had faith the size of a mustard seed, you would move mountains. With a little more patience you will benefit greater from pleasures of life. (Go to number 7)

86   Timeout.

Our goals and dreams are important to us so we always put a great deal of time and effort into achieving them. After a while we can almost become confused with thought. Situations might not be going according to plan. This can lead to frustration. Although frustration can be perceived as a good thing because it shows that we want more out of life, it can also create negative thoughts which will lead to failure. Take timeout. Today is your day off! Turn your attention onto happier thoughts. Put your feet up! Find something else to do for a while. The short break clears your mind of unnecessary thoughts that were clogging your mind and preventing you from finding a solution.

87   Compliment someone.

When was the last time that you complimented someone? Do you find it difficult to pay someone a compliment? A simple gesture can change someone's mood in an instant. They could have been having a bad day where nothing was working out. After you compliment them it will quickly return a smile back to their face. Comment on someone's: face, eyes, hair, clothes or their outline. You didn't really need me to give you any encouraging suggestions... did you?

88   Drown out negative thoughts.

Have you noticed how quickly a negative thought multiplies? It can easily multiply into a web of thoughts if we allow our minds to drift at will. Drown out a negative thought by concentrating on a positive one. Thinking of happy memories also helps to alleviate the pressure. Negative thoughts are like pop-ups on a computer. You can either leave them to slowly take over your screen or you can press delete to remove them. Be prepared though because they may be back at a later stage so you will have to delete them regularly.

89   Try another approach.

Are you becoming frustrated? There are times when we become completely exhausted from our efforts. The constant failed attempts taking our every strength to accept. Sometimes all it takes is to try another approach, which then opens up a variety of new opportunities. When you truly feel as though you have given it your best, be prepared to try another way.

90   Greet people with a smile.

When we are overwhelmed with negative thoughts it's only natural to frown. Our facial features are a true reflection of our inner thoughts. We don't realise that we are frowning because we are too busy trying to make sense of the recurring thoughts. Try to be aware of your surroundings at the same time as thinking, that way when you go to greet someone you can then rapidly persuade yourself to smile. It's a great habit that you can learn to control. Creating this habit enables you to check on a regular basis that you are prepared to approach other people... with a smile.

91   You are better than you think.

Several of your friends have told you that yet you still have not got enough confidence in yourself. You are only holding yourself back with that view of yourself. You have had plenty of self help suggestions and you should be well on your way to feeling better about yourself.

92   Life is one big road with lots of signs.

There are lots of signs to help us make the right choices. There are also signs that give us the wrong direction to go in. Don't drive so fast and you will have more time to read them. We don't have to go down the road all alone. There is help out there. We just need to take more time to decide which signs to follow. (Go to number 70)

93   I'm a go-getter.

Many people talk about what they need to do to become successful but only a small proportion actually do something about it. Businesses are built by people that have overcome the fear factor and are prepared to try and reach their goals and dreams. Show that you are business orientated. Get up and go for the ones that you really desire. He who tries, wins.

94   Everything will work out in the end.

At the present moment it probably feels as though there is no hope of us achieving our goals. It is as though we are wasting time pursuing something that we will never attain. Have faith in your abilities. At present it looks like you have not got much chance in succeeding but you will. Give it a little more time. Concentrate on the end result and eventually your efforts will materialise into your success.

95   They are making a big mistake.

It sounds like a fantastic idea, but they can't see it yet. Their vision isn't as clear as yours. You've thought it through in great detail and become more excited. The benefits are phenomenal so it is them that are making a big mistake. Give them more time and eventually they will see the benefits too.

96   There's a light at the end of the tunnel.

Have you run out of ideas? Are you desperate for help? When we reach to this stage, it feels as though we have entered a dark tunnel, not being able to see which direction to go in. When you carefully look far into the distance, you will see a small light of hope. Keep walking towards it and you will eventually get there.

97   Patience is a virtue.

Many problems that we experience are due to our lack of patience. We become engrossed with wanting issues solved immediately. There are certain procedures that have to be followed. Tasks can take longer than we first anticipated. There are also circumstances that are out of our control. Have a little more patience and you will see something happening soon.

98   Have a laugh.

A laugh a day, keeps the negative thoughts away. Indulging in laughter can easily change our mood from feeling frustrated to being happy again. Important chemicals in our body are released during laughter which can dramatically improve our health. Learn to laugh by thinking of something funny. It could be a cheerful memory or your favourite film. Some people find you irresistible when they see you laugh! Tickle yourself to make you laugh. If that doesn't work... tickle someone else!

99   Have good posture.

Walk with your shoulders back. Don't crouch because it can cause curvature of the spine. Enter a room looking straight ahead to appear more confident. Use your knowledge of body language to your advantage. Position yourself to appear more interested in what other people are saying.

100   Always give a %.

Attempting to deal with several tasks can cause us to put in less effort into each of them. The standard of work will end up being lower than if we only had a single item to deal with. Concentrate all your thoughts and emotions into every task. Try not to take on too much work at once. You can easily become confused with thought. It is better to complete one assignment than to nearly finish two.

101   Surprise a friend.

You should aim to take your eyes off yourself and think of other people at least once a month. How does it feel when someone close to you contacts you after several months of silence? They will feel just as excited when you contact them too. Do something that is completely out of your character as your new one is reshaped.

102   Appreciate what you can see.

When you look carefully you will see that the world is beautiful. Take more time to admire colourful flowers and butterflies and take a moment to observe the magnificent landscapes. Close your eyes for a few seconds and imagine that you no longer had the ability to see. What would you miss? Appreciate the beauties of the world while you still can.

103   If they can do it, I can do it.

We can sometimes admire people as though they are doing something that we can only dream of doing. Believe in your abilities. Other people are not superior to you. Their skills can be learnt. Be prepared to work extremely hard for meaningful goals. Having a positive attitude towards life will result in you achieving more success.

104   What's your dream?

Dreams can easily fade away when neglected. Our dreams are equivalent to the petrol in a car. As we drive along the long road of life, our petrol slowly runs out. It is imperative that we refuel at the next gas station or else we will no longer be able to go on any further. We need to constantly refuel our dreams too, because we won't get any further in life without them. Reach deeper down into your mind to build up your dreams. Refer to them on a regular basis so as not to run low. Make them more important to you by becoming more passionate about them.

105   Stop wishing.

Wishing for situations to improve or to sort themselves out doesn't work. People don't feel obliged to give you a better job and debt problems don't just go away by themselves, they only get worse. Do something about it. Go out and make things happen. Be prepared to work for what you desire. (Go to number 40)

106   Control.

Learn to control your thoughts, your emotions and your actions. It is very tempting to act on impulse. That is usually when we get ourselves into trouble and then suffer the consequences. We need to take more time before reacting. Our body language can also detect when people are losing control. In certain situations it is better to relax your arms down by the side of your body. It shows less aggression and will help to defuse a situation.

107   It's okay to be scared.

When a martial arts expert gains their black belt it signifies that they are classed as fearless. They are prepared for any confrontation with another human. That same person might turn out to be scared of a small puppy dog. We are all scared of something. Are you scared of approaching people? Have some answers ready for their wide range of responses. We are not usually scared of speaking to people, we are more worried about how to handle their responses. Use them as a learning tool and see them as your practice runs. If they disagree with your product, then you have learnt another way that doesn't work. Try it on someone else until you get a different response. (Go to number 3)

108   You're a winner.

You are a winner but when was the last time that you told someone else that they too are a winner? People need us to help pick them up when they are feeling low. Share some of your positive attitude with someone else. Help to keep them from thinking negatively about themselves.

109   They are jealous.

Are you having problems with other people's attitudes? Don't worry about what other people say. It usually turns out that they are jealous of you. They secretly wish that they had your happiness, your positive attitude and your success. Keep doing your best and take no notice of them. Next time you hear of someone complaining about you, smile because you know that they are just jealous.

110   I will find time.

We all have twenty-four hours in a day - unless you are a magician. Sometimes we complain of not having enough time. Then something else turns up and somehow – magically, we find time. Have you noticed? It's because you are more passionate about that particular issue. The more important goals and dreams are to you, the more likely that you will be prepared to find time. It is usually a small matter of readjusting a few tasks to make more time. (Go to number 65)

111   Courtesy.

Learning manners doesn't cost anything but it makes the world of difference between liking and disliking someone. First impressions last the longest so if you are polite, people will remember you for that. It is better to say 'thank you' too many times than not enough. Be helpful to less fortunate people. Control yourself and don't act immaturely when in public. When opening doors, look around to see if there is anyone behind you. Be prepared to hold the door open for people and don't always expect a positive response.

112   There are certain things that are out of our control.

You can attempt to take every precaution available to prevent an incident, yet it happens anyway. Unfortunately you don't rule the world. Sometimes when you are trying one way of handling a situation there are others trying to handle them differently. Learn to accept that things can't always go your way. Spend less time worrying about whether you could have done anything to avoid it. What is done has already been done and there is nothing that you can do to change it. It's time to move on.

113   Be consistent and persistent.

Rocks are able to withstand the frequent bombardment of water. After a long while of constantly brushing against the rock, the water will finally penetrate it. You need to keep trying even though you are tired of the constant knock backs. Be like water and eventually you will succeed.

114   Don't make a mountain out of a mole hill.

A simple problem can easily escalate if we allow it too. We try to find logical ways to explain the issue that we are experiencing. Then we share our views with other people. After a while what started off as a small problem is now considered to be almost life threatening. Learn to control your thoughts before they fragment out of control. Act on more important matters and dismiss trivial ones. (Go to number 34)

115   Lack of confidence leads to failure.

Have you given up on a challenge? If so then you will surely fail. You need to be confident. It is one of the most important ingredients of success. Once you have achieved enough self confidence, other challenges become easier. Find some ways to enhance your confidence. Certain clothes, shoes or even having your hair in a particular style helps to make people feel less self conscious. When you are confident, you believe that you have the ability to succeed where others have failed. Be confident. (Go to number 66)

116   Knowledge is power.

It is far easier to further your career with a higher level of education. There may be times where you have to force yourself to enrol on a college course but it is for your own good. Know your product by engaging in some research. Don't settle for working for someone else for the rest of your life. Educate yourself and become your own boss.

117   Yin Yang.

Hot and cold; hard and soft; fast and slow; light and dark; positive and negative. Nobody is all positive. We all have a little negative within us. If you are always rushing around it can lead you to feeling stressed. Slowing down for a while will help calm you down and relieve your anxiety. It's time to make some simple adjustments to your life. The key is to find the right balance to maintain a higher level of happiness. Don't moan about your problems all the time, but equally as important, don't keep all your problems to yourself. Learn to balance your life.

118   Life isn't fair.

We can be out working extremely hard at achieving our goals and dreams. Within an instant we can discover that we have inherited a life threatening disorder through no fault of our own. There are also people that appear to obtain success far easier than others. Life isn't fair but that isn't an excuse to give up pursuing your goals. Don't give in to temptation. Rummage through your mind to find ways of increasing your chances of success. (Go to number 85)

119   Time waits for nobody.

There are times where we decide to tackle an issue next week. Then when we look back we realise that a month has passed and we still haven't attempted to deal with it. Many people tend to procrastinate as though they have all the time in the world. Stop wasting time. Work hard while you are able, because if something were to go drastically wrong with your health that prevented you from completing a task, you will regret not taking it more seriously. (Go to number 29)

120   Be prepared.

It is easy to build up your confidence to be able to approach people. It is people's responses we need to be prepared for. Dealing with the variety of responses is similar to playing a game of chess. First you decide which piece you're going to move. Then you workout a strategy which will include the different counters that will become available. Then you prepare another move to counter their response. When you are confident with the series of strategic moves, you then take your first move. They then respond accordingly. You have already thought of a counter prior to taking your first move so you can confidently play on. An advanced chess player always thinks at least four moves ahead. Treat life as though you are playing a game of chess.

121   You never know until you try.

We can invent a thousand reasons why a particular task is destined to failure. Our past track record, the amount of obstacles we have encountered or the lack of support that we have received. The list is endless. After a while someone more positive comes along and persuades us to give it a try. We then end up succeeding. Learn to think of more positive reasons to excel in life. You have the ability to create a barrage of ideas to work on. They will keep your mind busy for a while. You will achieve more from merely trying more.

122   Learn to be more organised.

Do you wish that you had more hours in a day? Sometimes we have several tasks to complete but often feel as though there isn't enough time to finish them all. In most cases all it takes is for us to be more organised. Prioritise your tasks. Try to deal with several projects that are in the same area rather than making unnecessary journeys.

123   Duplicate yourself.

Are you struggling to cope on your own? There are times when we take on too much work and find it too much of a challenge to cope with it all. We then fall behind with completing important tasks. Find someone that you trust and train them up to be able to take the leadership role when ever necessary. Learn to share your work load.

124   I am what I think I am.

Are you a failure or are you a winner? You may come across a challenge that appears too difficult to overcome so you consider quitting. That doesn't mean that you are a failure. Find another way to tackle your situation. Learn to be confident and keep believing in your abilities. Using the phrase 'I was born a winner', will give you the extra fuel to drive you forwards. Are you a winner?

125 Multiply a happy thought.

You have already been advised on how to think of a happy thought, but sometimes a single thought isn't quite sufficient to drown out a multitude of negative ones. If you have a single happy thought to three mind draining negative ones, you need to imagine being in different situations using the single thought. Picture yourself enjoying the thought to the fullest. You can think of three different circumstances which will give you four happy thoughts to three negative ones. Thinking of a happy thought repeatedly works in the same way to alleviate the pressure of the negative ones. What started off as an almost depressing day can easily end up as a happy one. Learn to expand on cheerful thoughts by searching deeper into your mind.

126 Spare a thought for others.

It's that time of the month again! This is the period where we think of other people. Try not to neglect your family and friends. They may need some assistance with their goals too. Being thoughtful towards other people is another important ingredient necessary to increase your chances of success. Don't let your ego deter you from achieving your goals. Offer your assistance to other people and they will also become more positive. You can help to make our country a better place to live in by spreading your positive attitude on to other people.

127 I agree.

Would it really make that much difference to a particular situation for us to be right? Discussions can escalate out of control but afterwards we realise that our view wasn't that important. There's no harm with occasionally agreeing with others to avoid an argument. Do you agree?

128 Positive thoughts lead to positive actions.

We are governed by our thoughts. When we think negatively, we act accordingly. We are judged by our actions and not by our thoughts even though our actions are a direct result of our thoughts. Use mind control. Learn to consistently think positively and you will automatically act in a more positive manner. We can choose what to think of by practicing mind changing techniques. (Go to number 70)

129 Is it worth fighting for?

We have been consistently battling against all odds to achieve a particular goal. After a while we begin to lose hope because we have little to show for our loyal efforts. The uncomfortable feeling then creates frustration. How important is it to you? Don't be scared to reassess a situation. It could turn out that you simply needed to try alternative routes. (Go to number 86)

130 It's not what you say but what's in your heart that matters.

Has a particular person told you that they care about you but deep down you know that they don't? Words are cheap. They don't want to see you rich they would rather see you poor. Observe people's actions and not their verbal dialect. Ignore what they say because eventually their conscience will let them know that they are doing you wrong. There are people that lack communication skills but they would do practically anything for you.

131 Keep your mind busy.

Keeping our mind busy isn't easy as it has a multitude of automatic thoughts racing through our head all the time. Learn to override them by persistently selecting the thoughts to concentrate on. Choose what to think of especially when you are experiencing problems. Somehow you will have to deal with your challenges. They can drain all the positive energy out of you if you dedicate too much time to them. (Go to number 6)

132   Know your product.

It is a waste of time trying to move a product that you are not familiar with. People will question you on matters that you know little about. Learn to have confidence in your product by studying important facts and information that you may be asked to comment on. Prepare yourself to be questioned by having prejudged answers.

133   If you want positive advice, ask a positive person.

You already knew that, didn't you? Then why do so many of us regularly ask people with little or even no knowledge of the subject in question? There are many people that are experts at knowing a great deal about... nothing. Avoid acquiring advice from these people as it is always negative advice given that will put you off pursuing that particular idea. When you ask a positive person for advice, they will always say something positive, even if it's another angle to approach your goal. You will come away feeling more motivated than how you originally felt.

134   If you can't hear, you must feel.

This was my mother's favourite phrase. As a caring mother she would constantly advise us on how to live a happier life with minimal problems. My mother never forced her views upon us. She merely directed us on how to make fewer mistakes. It was now up to us which path we took. Are some of your family and friends trying to give you good advice? The choice is yours. Be prepared to suffer the consequences of your choices.

135   Don't dwell.

It would be great if everything worked out according to our plans. Unfortunately life doesn't work like that. We experience situations where we are dissatisfied with the results. Then we replay the series of actions leading up to the end result. They then create a multitude of negative thoughts which slowly spreads throughout our mind. It causes us to act accordingly and soon we find ourselves constantly complaining and moaning about a situation that couldn't have been avoided. I urge you to put it all down to experience and move on. The longer you spend thinking about it, the worse you will feel. (Go to number 26)

136   It's acceptable to feel like quitting.

When you have put adequate efforts into your goals without much sign of success, it is all too normal to consider quitting. Have your moment of despair but be aware of the level of negative thoughts present within your mind. Take some time out if you desperately need to. You can even say that you quit, but don't actually give up. (Go to number 129)

137   Negativity eats away at us like a virus.

It can start off as a single thought that grows to a level that it is forced to split into two. They both grow and split and multiply. The mass of negative thoughts begins to eat away your positive ones, leaving you looking like a zombie. Before you know it, what started off as an inkling has now manifested into a deadly disease. Negative thoughts are highly infectious so you are advised to stay well clear of them. If you have already been infected then you are in need of some medicine. The special antibiotics will rebuild your body's immune system to a level that can withstand the negative influences. (Go to number 125)

138   Enhance your memory.

You can learn to remember important facts and information by first convincing yourself that you have an excellent memory. Create a habit of assigning people's names to a name of someone close to you. Visualise them as the one stored in your long term memory. Another way to recall people's names is to run through the alphabet and recite people's names for each letter. Learn to memorise phone numbers by breaking them up into smaller numbers that you are more familiar with. Repeat it several times to help to remember. Create ridiculous stories to remember a series of events. The more passion you put in, the more likely you'll remember.

139   Tell jokes.

Although many people view humour as an indication of a shallow mind, it can also be a clever way of embracing challenges. When we encounter too many problems, we are left with the choice whether to laugh or cry. Jokes create laughter, which releases endorphins that promote happiness. This then leads to us feeling more positive about dealing with our problems. Create a sense of humour and tell some jokes.

140   Be sympathetic.

There will come a time where certain friends and family will be in need of emotional support. It is your job to be able to recognise the early signs. Their change in personality, the lack of empathy in their words or their emotional state are a few. Take other people's feelings into consideration. Don't pretend to hear, actually take time to listen to their dissatisfactions. You might learn something about them that can positively change your initial views of them.

141 On the way to success there's always someone trying to put you off.

It can start off as though their concerns are genuine, but as time goes on it becomes obvious that they are adamant to put you off. Their advice becomes a desperate order as though they are well educated in that particular field. Have they got the knowledge? Be aware that most of the time it is just a smoke screen. They don't know what they are talking about so seek advice from another more reliable source. (Go to number 109)

142 Motivate yourself.

You can't always expect other people to help inspire you. Sometimes you have to learn how to motivate yourselves. Create situations within your mind that promote positive actions. Visualise yourself in more positive circumstances. Believe in your ability to succeed. Imagine how you would feel to accomplish all your goals and dreams. Have the confidence to see yourself failing. This will feel so uncomfortable that you will push yourself even harder to make sure that you succeed. Internal motivation can be developed from a single thought. Find more ways to motivate yourself.

143 External motivation.

Use the influence of other people to help motivate you. Find out what motivates them to act in a more positive fashion. Learn how to simulate their actions. Try to be around more enthusiastic people so that you have a positive attitude towards life. Attend motivational seminars as they will boost your self confidence.

144   Be aware of your surroundings.

There is a great deal that you can learn from observing your surroundings. When you look closely you can see the various human behaviourisms at work. Certain people act differently depending on the circumstances. You can easily select which attitudes to follow and which ones to avoid. Observing people's actions can help you react quicker which also makes you appear more assertive. This will enhance your perception and people will see you as being more considerate as you almost seem to read their minds.

145   It's a sin to waste a good talent.

There are people that appear to be a natural at particular activities. We consider them to be talented. To see people waste their talent is almost painful to imagine. If you already have or you have skilfully developed an ability that other people simply envy, refrain from misusing it. Put it to good use. Don't waste your abilities.

146   Don't jump to conclusions.

When we walk into a room and somebody laughs, it doesn't mean that they are laughing at us. It is more probable that it was coincidental. They were probably engrossed in a conversation prior to us entering the room. If we allow ourselves to systematically act on impulse, we can soon become paranoid. Whenever a situation arises that leads you to a chain of thoughts, allow yourself enough time to come to the right conclusion. (Go to number 88)

147   We all have a point in which we can't go beyond.

We all have different stress levels where we will finally crack up. A house built using bricks can withstand a massive amount of pressure compared to a feeble house built from sticks. The house made from bricks has mortar to hold each brick firmly together. On the inside there is also another layer of brickwork to reinforce stability. During most storms this type of house can easily withstand the pressures exerted by the high winds. During freak storms where the wind exceeds the stress level of the house, you will see the brickwork beginning to crumble. Reinforce your mind using the immense power of positive thinking so that you can withstand a higher level of stress.

148   There is only a thin line between success and failure.

It can all depend on a single decision. A crucial point where you have the choice to finally give up after an impressive attempt of moving ahead, or reluctantly trying one last time which turns out to be the one that moves you on to the next step on the ladder of success. We can unknowingly give up one step short of a life changing decision, so have a little more faith and keep going.

149   Use your common sense.

We all know people that seem to act on impulse or psycho analyse simple issues. They fail to see the domino effects of their actions. They are fast to give their views but slow at reacting when a situation becomes worse. There are times when we should do and say the obvious, rather than seeking an in-depth explanation.

150   Count to five before you answer.

When you are faced with a challenge that requires a response, give yourself a little more time before reacting. Just a few seconds pause can easily defuse a situation that was building up to you exploding. It's amazing how much more calm you will become after counting to five before responding. A short delay that creates silence will also persuade people to take more notice of what you are saying. Try it today.

151   Don't let people walk all over you.

I know that you are a kind hearted person but they do too. They trust and need you to uplift them over the obstacles that they are experiencing. They begin to ask you for your help and support so often that they begin to expect it. Slowly but surely they forget that you are actually doing them a favour. Before you know it, you're regularly putting their needs before your own. Don't let people take advantage of your kindness. Learn to say 'No'. You need to be confident enough to deal with the situation as it can eat away at your self esteem.

152   Phone a friend.

Can you think of someone to contact that you haven't spoken to for a while? They will probably say to you that they were thinking about you just before you called them. This is due to our split second thoughts that we experience every few minutes of each day. It's great to know that other people are thinking about us for a short while of each day! Contact someone today.

153   Businesses are built on thin threads.

We start off struggling to find the finances to get it started. Then we passionately work hard to develop our revenue with little to show for our efforts. We then sacrifice our spare time to put an adequate amount of hours in. We encounter rejection on a regular basis that tempts us on many occasions to quit. Even our close friends and some family members try to discourage us until we feel as though we are all alone. It feels as though we are the only one to see the real benefits that it will have on us and our family. After a long, hard struggle of overcoming our challenges, we finally succeed. Be prepared to work hard for what you want.

154   Use incentives.

Business might not be going according to your predictions and you are probably experiencing a little frustration. Offer your staff incentives to encourage them to become more productive and dedicated. Try and persuade them to concentrate on the incentive and not the work. The incentive to them is a goal and if they are serious enough about a goal, they will find a way of achieving them. Depending on the type of business you are involved in, you may well have to offer your customers incentives to encourage repeat business.

155   Trust your instincts.

A clever thought pops into our mind and it seems so obvious. We then question ourselves by analysing our thought in greater detail. In just a short space of time we complicate a simple idea. It then leads us to a different conclusion. After a while we find out that our original thought was the correct one. In simple situations, trust your instincts.

156   Perseverance.

Success can seem to almost take forever. It is equivalent to running a marathon. The majority of people won't even contemplate entering the race due to fear of failure - or maybe they are too unfit to run such a distance! The ambitious few take a risk and the race begins. There are a few that start off fast but they soon slow down after a few miles. Most people pace themselves and run at an average speed. The challenge of the hills takes a great deal out of people but they continue. You come across unlevelled grounds where your ankle becomes painful from the constant readjustments. After a short while you come across another hill which strains your ankle and begins to wear out your quad muscles but you persevere. After another short while it begins to rain which adds to your discomfort. You come across a slope and you feel the pain in your knees. Then the challenge of another hill takes too much strength out of you and you become tired. Your mind begins to drift and you wonder whether it is worth the pain but you convince yourself to continue once more. After a few more miles you pass someone that informs you that you are only half way. You can't believe that you still have a great distance to run and you become despondent. It becomes too much pressure on your mind and body so you choose to take timeout and walk. The battle begins in your mind whether to give up or persevere. You feel all your muscles tightening up and draining away your strength. The moment comes where you decide whether to give up or go on before your muscles becomes too tight for you to run anymore. You find the strength once more to run on. A few more hills take it out on your quads but you run on. The wind begins to blow hard but you continue. The pain and stress on your body becomes almost too much to handle, but you choose to run on. After another while of battling against yourself whether to give up, you realise that... you have finished the race. Somehow through all the challenges you managed to persevere to the end.

157   Things can only get better.

Imagine having an awesome party with lots of people eating and drinking and generally enjoying themselves. The next morning though, you wake up to see the aftermath. You stand there and view the destructive mess left behind for you to clean up. It looks like an impossible task that could take forever. You don't even know where to start. The attitude you must have is to see it at the worst that it could be. Start with an item close to you. Then continue with putting out the rubbish. After a while you will be able to see a path through to the kitchen. A few more moments pass and you are able to see an end to your ordeal, and before you know it you will be back on your feet.

158   Do you really want it?

Do you? Are you prepared to work hard enough to achieve it? Yes you are! You are experiencing feelings that are considered as normal under the circumstances. It's fine to feel dissatisfied with the cards that you have been dealt. You can choose to fold now before you make a fool of yourself, or take a risk and play on. The fun seems to have disappeared so it's time to find it again to encourage you to keep trying. (Go to number 115)

159   Be friendly.

It is very tempting to give people a piece of your mind especially when they show you lack of consideration. Some people don't think before they speak and end up showing lack of manners. They have not being taught how to deal with other people in various situations, but you have. Therefore it is up to you to take the initiative and show your people skills. Using the phrases 'Thank you' or 'Please' is a great way of showing people that their lack of manners has failed to affect the way you speak to them. (Go to number 44)

160   Just do it.

If you believe in yourself, you can do anything. Many of you pass your driving test but are afraid to drive on the motorway. You are afraid of the increased speed and volume of traffic. When you passed your driving test it qualified you to be able to cope with the stress and pressures of these circumstances. After you have persuaded yourself to try it once, the next time you attempt it you will feel less nervous. After a while you will wonder why you were so apprehensive in the first place.

161   Everyone makes mistakes.

During our game of chess we anticipate our opponent's moves. We try our best to stay one step ahead with our strategic thoughts. As the game becomes more intense we neglect a few obvious signs and begin to concentrate on particular pieces. We concentrate so much that we almost adopt tunnel vision to overcome those pieces. Our opponent makes an unorthodox move with a piece that is out of our focus range. Before you know it we are on the defensive. After a while of countering the various challenges, we run into trouble and they force us into a checkmate. The good news is that we are playing the chess version of the game of life where we have the choice to quit or play on by removing the offending piece.

162   Learn how to meditate.

We can become so worked up with stress that we encounter, that we feel as though we are about to explode. Meditation is a way of switching off our thoughts for a short while to give us a chance to cool down. Even the most sophisticated cars can overheat, so what makes you think that we can cope with continual pressure forever? We all need an occasional break from our obsessive thoughts. Relax by manoeuvring yourself into a comfortable position. Shut yourself away from the real world by closing your eyes for a short moment. Most thoughts are created from what we see. Breathe in and out through your nose to cleanse the air. Try to empty your mind of the conflicting thoughts. Although silence is an excellent state to achieve, you may also hum to help filter your thoughts. Monks meditate the most and frequently resort to humming. You will be amazed with the benefits a mere few minutes of meditation makes. Start with just a few seconds each day and then build up from there. Thai-Chi is also another way of relaxing. It de-stresses your mind and body. (Go to number 68)

163   Learn to say NO.

People tend to take advantage of your kindness, especially when they know that you always say 'Yes.' When you give them an inch they want a mile. They will keep asking until you find the confidence to say 'No.' It is harder to stand up for yourself when you lack confidence and feel insecure. Some people take note of your inabilities and will eventually take advantage of you. If you struggle to turn them down, don't be hesitant to ask a trusted friend to represent your views. Eventually you will have to represent yourself or else they will keep asking. (Go to number 42)

164   Enjoy the chase.

Life can be fun when you are in the right frame of mind. You can choose which goals to pursue and work out different strategies to gain them. You can dedicate as much time and effort into them as you wish but at the same time do not feel disappointed if you fail to achieve them. A cat seems to enjoy chasing rats but when they fail to catch them, they find another one to play with. Find some goals to chase after and make it your mission to keep trying until you succeed.

165   Take care of your health.

What use is success if you can't enjoy it due to ill health? It seams as though we pay more attention to our cars than our own health. Cars have a yearly MOT. We also service them regularly to prevent breakdowns, changing the oil and other major parts that rapidly wear out. We even take some pride in its appearance and make sure that it always looks clean. If we put the same effort into making sure that our bodily functions are in good working order, we too would have fewer breakdowns. Take care of your body as though it's more important than your car.

166   Reap what you sow.

The first stage is to educate ourselves on the type of seeds that will grow to our desired size. We then need to spend money on purchasing our selected seeds. Then we need to bury them in some fertilised soil. Rather than leaving them and hoping for the best, we must then regularly attend to them, watering, feeding and nursing them whenever necessary. After a long while we can enjoy seeing them grow according to our plans. Now we will reap the rewards of our efforts.

167 When it rains it pours.

It starts off as a drizzle and you feel brave enough to cope without using your umbrella. You casually walk on towards your destination without showing much signs of being affected by the pitiful rain. Dealing with it is quite easy but as time goes on the light rain becomes heavier. Despite your efforts to cope, you become wet and uncomfortable. The rain clouds your vision and you struggle to focus on where you are going. You try a little longer but soon have to resort to using your umbrella. After another short while, the rain beats down hard against your umbrella until you feel yourself fighting hard to hold onto it. You hold on tight to the handle but the rain coupled with the immense wind, becomes too fierce and blows your umbrella inside out. Once again you are exposed to the heavy rain and your clothes become drenched. In the soaking rain you attempt to fix your umbrella to no avail because after another while of fighting against the combination of the wind and rain, the problem with your umbrella repeats itself. You consider seeking shelter but as you attempt to wipe away some of the rain from your eyes, you realise that you are on your own. Then almost out of nowhere comes a large truck that sprays water from a puddle in the road, all over you. Frustrated and damp, you hastily walk on. The rain becomes so heavy that it produces large puddles on the pavement that you struggle to see. In your haste you accidentally step in one. It turns out to be deep and soaks your shoes and socks. You look down at your shoes in disgust, your trousers and top sticking to your damp skin. With the rain dripping from your nose by the bucket full, you look up to see that the rain doesn't show any sign of slowing down. Finally you reach your destination only to encounter your next problem. It's closed due to the heavy rain! How do you feel now? Confused with thought, you start on your return journey home but this time you concentrate hard on finding refuge from the rain. In the distance you notice a bus shelter that seemed ample enough to protect you from the rain. After a few minutes of taking shelter and having some time out, almost like magic, the rain stops and the sun comes out. Although it might not seem it at the time, eventually the sun will shine through the dark clouds of rain.

Be prepared to take on several problems at once.

168   Give constructive criticism.

How do you feel when people criticise you? It is difficult to accept the possibility that you may be wrong. Sometimes you feel so intense with emotions that you may even consider quitting. Whenever you criticise other people, be more tactful with your choice of words. Try to help them feel better of themselves before you carefully give them guidance of how to improve. Then always finish off with a positive word of advice to help build their confidence once more.

169   I will always be there for you.

When was the last time you said that to someone? There are a few of your friends that feel discouraged because of the bad hand of cards that they have been dealt with in life. They have tried to make the correct decisions based on their hand but the next card they are dealt is equally as upsetting. It can almost appear as though they are consistent in making incorrect choices but it is actually through no fault of their own. Be thoughtful and uplift them with a gentle phrase that reminds them that you are there whenever they might need you. A simple word of encouragement will make the world of difference to other people.

170   Look in the mirror.

When you look in the mirror as you move a limb, your reflection follows your actions. If you speak your reflection copies what you say. When you give advice, be prepared to refer to it when you are faced with a similar situation. There are people that are experts at giving advice, yet when they are faced with an equivalent situation they fail to follow suit. Next time you are interested in sharing your wisdom, imagine someone giving you the same advice.

171 Forget the past.

We all have an issue in the past that we would rather forget about. It could be an issue that we have grown to realise we handled it incorrectly. Maybe it's an issue involving someone else that previously affected us. The past can haunt us if we allow our minds to drift at will. The thoughts can escalate out of control and drive us to a multitude of conclusions. The vivid thoughts can also affect our actions that we will regret later on in life. The less we think about the past, the easier it is to concentrate on our future.

172 Don't put all your eggs in one basket.

It is not wise to collect all your eggs up in to one basket as you may trip and fall breaking them all in one go. Carry your eggs in several baskets so if you have problems with breaking all the eggs in one basket, you would have other baskets of eggs to carry back on a later date. Treat your dreams and goals as though they are baskets of eggs. It's less painful that way. Have several to work towards and if one fails, try another one.

173 Focus.

It's very easy to become distracted from our main priority. Our attention can be diverted to other issues that are happening around us. Our interest grows as a chain of thoughts builds up within our mind. Learn the art of redirecting your thoughts back to your original mission. Refer to your main priority on a regular basis, so as not to become too indulged in trivial matters. Set your eyes firmly on your goals and maintain your composure.

174 You can lead a horse to water but you can't force it to drink from it.

You have grown into an ambitious person who can see the positive aspects in most situations. The benefits are overwhelmingly obvious to you as your tunnel vision is now cured. Sharing your views with other people is far from easy, as their vision isn't as clear as yours. Some people are sceptical, while others are ridiculously cynical. Try to think back to when you lacked confidence. You too were self conscious to a certain degree. After a long process of building up your self confidence, you are now strong enough to withstand the devastating criticisms and numerous rejections from other people. Be gentle, caring and patient. Work on their insecurities and soon they will become strong and confident. When this transformation is complete, they too will develop the diverse vision to see the benefits of drinking the water.

175 One step at a time.

As you climb up the ladder of success, you will feel as though your problems are getting worse. The strain on your muscles becomes more intense as you climb higher. You can easily become confused with thought and become increasingly hesitant with each step. Your perception towards your challenges will positively change when you take your eyes off yourself and focus on your goals. The hardest step was the first and if you look carefully, you will see your goals getting closer with every step you take. When you learn to concentrate on your goals, the pain of each step fades away.

176   Nobody's perfect.

As a mediocre basketball player you were only succeeding to score once in every ten attempts. You made the decision to become an expert player by practicing with every spare moment you have. In your practice sessions you improved to a remarkable level, scoring all ten basketballs in the net first time. You maintained your high standard throughout the league and progressed with your team into the finals. The team that you are competing against skilfully beat the defending champions. They are one point ahead with only a few seconds to go before the end of the match. Under the intense pressure you miss a single shot that would have given your team a well deserved draw. Your almost perfect track record shattered at the end of the most important game of the season. Within days of that crucial match, you return to practice but under more intense pressure. Perfection doesn't exist. However small, there is always room for improvement.

177   Things could be worse.

When things go wrong we have a tendency to think that it's the end of the world. We think that our problems are the worst. It would be great to have more situations turn out according to plan but life isn't that simple. The same situation we are complaining about could have turned out even worse. We still have the chance to improve certain aspects even though we would have preferred a different outcome. Make the best of what cards life has dealt you.

178 Limit your negative input.

Refer to negative information as though it's a dripping tap. Your plug is in the sink and the water is dripping very slowly from the tap. The first few drips don't even make an impact on your mind but sure enough as time goes on, the sink will fill with water. Negative information clogs your mind in a similar manner. You need to create an outlet to drain away the negative waste before it becomes overpowering. Refrain from becoming too confident because as long as the plug is still in, the sink will eventually overflow. It's at this stage where you become too stressed and you may even show signs of depression. Tighten the tap so that it can't drip by staying away from too many negative people. (Go to number 6)

179 Be a peace maker.

Do you know of someone that is in desperate need for an anger management course? We can all lose our temper if we are pushed to our limit. The point where we become angry and emotional and say things that is totally out of our character. Work on your control so that it takes more to push you to that undesirable point. Redirect your thoughts to avoid a negative build up. Defuse the atmosphere by changing your body language to appear less aggressive. Speak in a manner that shows you are confident but are not there for confrontation. Work on yourself first then encourage other people to adopt your peaceful attitude towards life.

180 Be hungry for success.

When we become hungry for food we go and find something to eat. The hungrier we become the more food we desire and the harder it is for us to resist. Create the need for success by managing your thoughts. Magnify your reasons why your goals are important to you. Focus on them until it almost feels painful not having them. A strategy must then be formulated prior to your quest for more, to minimize mistakes. Then attack your goals like a savage until you eat them all up.

181   Work on your communication skills.

The more confident you feel, the easier you will find it to speak to people. It also helps when you know what to say in the various situations. When you first greet people, force yourself to smile. Then add a little humour into your speech. Instead of saying 'Hello,' say 'Hello there,' or 'Hello young man or young lady.' That works very well on older citizens and always creates a smile on their faces! Practice parts of your speech on unsuspecting clients before using them on business candidates; like using an approach similar to; 'Excuse me, can you help me?' or 'Hello, my name is.' Try to make more general conversation with other people to build up your confidence when dealing with people. Creating laughter during a conversation also leads to other people feeling more relaxed around you. Be prepared to start a conversation rather than waiting for them to make the initial contact. First impressions last the longest.

182   Have a positive attitude on the phone.

Have you noticed that the way you are feeling at a particular time of the day mirrors the way you answer the phone? Having good communication skills can also be stretched to your manner on the phone. When answering the phone, prepare yourself before you pick up your receiver. Answer the phone with excitement. Think of a funny situation to encourage yourself to answer more cheerfully. Have a few scripts prepared in your mind in advance, for example 'good after morning', 'good after evening', 'Who's speaking please', 'can I help you?' Be aware of your tone of voice which can easily portray your attitude. I have been admired several times for my pleasant phone manner and people have even called me back just to thank me for cheering them up. Spice up the way you speak on the phone.

183   Be approachable.

You have developed excellent communication skills to start a conversation but sometimes people may require approaching you first. They might need your help and advice without your knowledge. Prior to speaking to you they will observe your posture and body language. They will ask for assistance from you over selecting someone else because you seem friendlier than the other people around. You are advised to bear that in mind when trying to encourage people to approach you.

184   Take no notice of gossip.

Some people thrive off gossip. They hear it and then enjoy spreading it to other people. They act as though they would grow old and grey if they were prevented from sharing it. When it's about other people it can almost feel satisfying but when it's about you, it can feel very hurtful. Some people can become emotional to a degree that causes them to have an inferior complex. It is sometimes known as Chinese whispers, where it starts off as a small insignificant issue. Then after it has been passed through a series of people and blown out of proportion, it is revealed as a devastating issue that needs immediate attention. It can also be a private problem that leads to other people needing medical attention for the excessive stress caused. Don't indulge in idle gossip and don't allow it to deter you from achieving more out of life. Gossip is irresistible but hurts on every level.

185   O.P.E. – other people's experience.

Sometimes we are seeking ways of diversifying a business but we are not sure how to develop it. We then ask a friend that knows everything about nothing! Most of the information they give us will be negative, which slowly diminishes the drive for success that we had. When you ask someone with proficient knowledge and experience in a particular field, you will get a better response. There are many other ways that you can learn from other people. Observing people's actions in certain situations can inspire you. Listening to other people can create useful ideas in your mind. You can also use other people's experience when giving positive advice by referring to their experience and not just your own views. There is a great deal to learn from other people.

186   Treat someone else.

You have already treated yourself and deserved every ounce of the enjoyment, now it's time to treat someone else. Go on; think of someone. There must be a friend or a family member that deserves a little treat. It doesn't have to be anything extravagant. Sometimes it's the small things that count.

187 Don't let your mind drift.

Our brain is capable of processing hundreds of different information at the same time. Within a split second we can have lots of different thoughts. Some we remember and others we forget until we are faced with a similar situation which sparks off the memory. Our minds can centre on thoughts that are not important at that moment in time. Then the thought manifests into a huge problem. Issues that were once priority becomes secondary and our minds are diverted to unimportant tasks. Before you know it you are well behind with your primary issue. We then try and piece together the limited information and concentrate on finding solutions. After a while we realise that we have been concentrating on an issue that can be left until another time. Find other ways to refocus. Learn how to recognise when your mind begins to drift. Be prepared to consistently divert your thoughts to your primary tasks.

188 Don't ask negative people for advice.

Why do we punish ourselves by asking negative people for advice on matters that they have no valid knowledge? It's easily done as there is a great deal of them all around us. We wouldn't ask someone for directions if we knew they were not from around that area of the country. They would surely send us off in the wrong direction. Negative people will send you in the wrong direction too. They will direct you towards failure instead of towards the road of success.

189 Be excited.

Have you noticed that certain people appear to be able to sell almost anything? When you observe them closely you will learn how they do so. They are excited about the product. Their tone of voice encourages you to want to hear more. Use your knowledge of body language to your advantage. Wave your hands around more vigorously, smile and even repeat words to express them further.

190   Team work.

Football teams are made up of eleven individual experts. Each of them highly proficient in their specific positions, trained to a level that their actions becomes instinctive. When acting as a team they also need to know what other people are thinking. This is where their ability to anticipate other people's actions can lack knowledge and result in losing even though their team is made up of the best individual players. Find out more about other people's strengths and weaknesses. Learn to anticipate when you will be needed. Encourage your team to act together as one and not as lots of individuals. Aim to work towards the same goal and eventually you will win.

191   End everyday happy.

During our everyday we experience both good and bad news. Many of us focus on the tragedies that are happening yet there are also positive incidences happening in front of us without us being able to see them clearly. There are times when we see the good things but then we still choose to concentrate on a problem that is more likely to end negatively. Enjoy a day that brings you good luck. When you have another task to deal with that is more likely to cause you more stress than relief, leave it until tomorrow. The calmer you are the more likely you will sleep. End your day happier and you will feel less anxious at night, which then leads to you having a more comfortable sleep. It is tempting to fit in as much as you can in a day but it is better to end your day feeling happy.

192   Take risks.

For several months other people have been trying to put you off chasing after one of your goals but you are not content. You want more out of life and your friends are not helping you progress to the next level. What have you got to lose? Don't be complacent, be hungry for success. Expand your mind. Picture yourself succeeding to increase your will to win. (Go to number 10)

193 Everyone has emotions.

We all experience different emotions at various times in our lives. Some of us hide them so that other people can't see them on the outside but we are still experiencing the pain on the inside. Showing your emotions is not a sign of weakness. You are normal to experience frustration, anger and sorrow. You can't be happy all of the time so learn to stop feeling as though you are useless just because you are being emotional. Have your moment then when you feel as though you have had enough divert your thoughts to an appropriate subject.

194 Learn to enjoy a challenge.

Our challenges are similar to completing a jigsaw puzzle. It can be completed because all the pieces are there. Your first problem is fitting them all together. You can't see it yet but when the jigsaw puzzle is completed the picture it forms is beautiful. As the picture begins to form you should become increasingly excited because you know that it will be worth the stress caused on the way. Your second problem is that there are more jigsaw puzzles to complete. Some of you are given harder ones to complete but the pictures that they produce are more radiant. Once you have completed your last jigsaw puzzle you will have reached your goal. Be prepared for a challenge. Are you ready? Say 'I was born ready!'

195   Venture out of your comfort zone.

It has been said that 95% of us work for someone else. We have a set routine where we work and then we get paid. It's very comfortable because we know after each week that we work we will get paid. Our bills and other important tasks in our lives can easily be planned as we know exactly how much money we have each week. Owning your own business is much more complicated. You have no idea of how much money you will bring in each week so most of us will feel very uncomfortable being in that type of situation. Although 95% of us know when we will be paid many of us desire more money to live a more comfortable life. Some of us admire the lifestyle of people that own their own businesses. Sometimes we wish that we had just a little more success but we are too afraid of venturing out of our comfort zone. People that have what you desire will tell you that feeling uncomfortable for a while is worth the pleasures it produces in the end. An entrepreneur works and works and works, then gets paid. The beauty of this concept is as time goes on you get paid more rapidly until you are hardly working and getting paid an extortionate amount. We all feel uncomfortable doing something but it will be worth the discomfort in the end.

196   Stay out of other people's comfort zone.

How do you feel when people get too close to you? People can become so engrossed in conversation that they don't realise they are constantly moving closer to you as they speak. Your sense of touch becomes aware of the air that is moving between you. It becomes difficult to avoid constant eye contact and you eventually feel uncomfortable. When other people are walking close your senses become alert and you may slow down to create more space between you. It is almost instinctive to keep people out of your comfort zone when dancing or waiting in a queue. It is fair to say that if you experience discomfort, then other people will also feel the same when your roles are reversed. Be aware of other people's comfort zone especially when you are having a heated discussion. Your ability to take other people into consideration can lead to defusing a situation.

197   Try to maintain eye contact.

Your eyes are like a window to your soul. They show whether you have a confident personality or if you are self conscious. It can show whether you are tired, disappointed, unhappy, shy or excited. Observing people's eyes can show you what they are thinking. Boxers use this method to anticipate their opponent's actions. Looking at the eyes can show when people have something to hide. Your eyes can also detect some illnesses by the change of shape or colour. Maintaining eye contact during a conversation allows people to feel as though you are more interested in their speech.

198   Don't judge a book by its cover.

A toad looks like a frog but it is of the lizard family. The cover of a book may not appeal to you. Its colour, texture and appearance may dissuade you from purchasing it. Once you have read the contents, your views of the book can drastically change. Don't judge other people solely by their appearance. People that seem more trustworthy from their appearance may turn out to be a bad choice of character. People that you first thought about avoiding may also turn out to be your most trusted friend. Give people a chance by getting to know them first. Don't prejudge people based on their appearance. Beauty is only skin deep. Beauty fades away but personalities can last forever.

199   Learn from your mistakes.

Everyone makes mistakes, you already know that. Most of us have driven a car while in the red. Some of you choose to complete your desired journey although you are quite aware that the petrol is running dangerously low. Most of you make it to a petrol station to refuel but some of you misjudge the miles left in your tank and run out of petrol unexpectedly. It can be an embarrassing experience, depending on where you break down. Your miscalculations should lead you to next time refuelling earlier or even avoiding driving while in the red or you have learnt nothing. Don't make the same mistakes again.

200   Think yourself to sleep.

Our days are full of action, packed with a multitude of tasks and issues to deal with. We can choose a particular task to think about as we go to sleep so that our mind works out a solution during the night. When you have several negative issues to deal with, choose a more cheerful thought to fall asleep to. Your mind will drift to other thoughts - mostly negative, that are plaguing your mind. It will be necessary to constantly redirect your thoughts until your positive thoughts are multiplied to a level that squeezes out the negative ones.

201   My problems are trivial.

It's not easy to imagine that our problems are trivial. We have been suffering for a long time, attempting to overcome them but failing everytime. It takes up most of our time trying to deal with them so how are we supposed to view them as trivial? Look around you and you will see the answers. There are people out there that have failed to leave a hospital for months due to ill health. You will see people with crippling disabilities that are learning to embrace them without complaining about the mental pain that they are experiencing. There are people who have terminal cancer with only a few more months to live. It's scary and will be extremely difficult to accept, but when you compare some of those severe problems to yours, you will realise that your problems are trivial in comparison. Learn to deal with your problems rather than constantly complaining about them.

202   Praise people for their efforts.

It is a very warming feeling to have someone sing your praises. The simple compliment boosts your ego and will drive you to accomplish greater things. You will give people a confidence boost when you pass on the same words of encouragement. It's amazing how much more we can achieve simply by feeling more highly of ourselves.

203   Make time.

We are all busy to an extent. Some of us more busy than others. It's not an acceptable excuse for our lack of compassion towards important issues in our lives. Make a point of readjusting a few aspects of your life to cater for your children, family and close friends. You may regret it if you accidentally lose them while you were too busy to make time to attend to them. In situations similar to this people develop a guilty conscience. You can avoid this emotion simply by making more time for them, now.

204   Good things come to those who wait, but they come faster to those who work for them.

Our local job centre sends us job vacancies relevant to our chosen career. Waiting for the right job can take a long time but eventually they will send information on a vacancy that appeals to us. A quicker and more efficient way to attain a job is to get out and look for one. There are always other vacancies at the job centre that they have failed to send us but we will be interested in. We can also buy a newspaper which will contain even more job vacancies. We are sure to obtain a job much faster by going out and searching for one. It is good to have patience but if you really want something, be prepared to work that little bit harder for it.

205   There are lots of signs in life.

Some signs appear bright and clear and point us in the right direction. There are signs that seem more appealing towards us but after we have finished reading them we will realise that they were misleading. Most of the signs are dull and hard to read but contain information to guide us on our journey towards success. There are also caution signs to help us on our way. These signs help us avoid the obstacles ahead of us by diverting us onto a safer route. They are written in a completely different colour that almost hurts our eyes to look at. It's those signs that we fail to take notice of but are the ones that we need the most. Be careful which signs you choose to follow.

206   Are you going to let someone put you off?

How important are your goals to you? Some people criticise everything whether it's something good or bad. They don't take your emotions into consideration and comment without taking time to realise how important it is to you. Are they prepared to assist you or put in the work for you? During your journey towards success you will meet many people that almost have a sole purpose to put you off. Avoid these people as much as possible.

207   You can't kid a kidder.

Certain people experience situations that shape their personalities. Their previous experience helps them become more assertive and perceptive towards other people that are going through similar situations. You may feel as though you can mislead them with your cunning responses but they will react to your every move. You may as well explain your true feelings as you will be only misleading yourselves.

208   Be determined.

A game of monopoly starts off as fun. It's exciting at the beginning because you are winning. As the game goes on you begin to make many mistakes and land on the wrong sections of the board. After a few hours of constantly paying for your mistakes, you reach a point where the game is no longer fun. It takes a great deal out of you but you are determined to see the game to the end. You choose to take a risk and put property onto your limited land. After a short while it pays off as several of the other players repeatedly land on your expensive property. In the end - after many painful hours, you will finally win.

209   Practice.

You have been taught many techniques including strategies on how to improve your confidence, body language and communication skills. Nobody can remember everything and as time goes on you will forget even more. The more you practice, the more information you are able to retain. Practice in your mind whenever you have a spare moment. Go through the series of steps laid out. Get used to practicing on your family and friends until it becomes an automatic response. The more you put in, the more success and confidence you will achieve.

210   Verbal conflict is a waste of words.

Some discussions can get out of hand and lead to arguments. They can sometimes be in public places where we attract attention. This can then lead to embarrassment. Learn control by refraining from acting on impulse. Verbal conflicts don't solve anything but fuel anger. If you know an angry person, maybe it's time they enrolled on an anger management program. The older you become the more mature you should be. It doesn't look good to act immature around children because it shows a negative way of handling situations. Show them good morals. Show them who is more grown up by walking away.

211   Fix up.

We can sometimes make choices that eventually lead to destruction. It is then easier to blame other people for our mistakes. We can wallow and moan about a particular situation that resulted from our lack of wisdom. There were times where we could have tried to deal with our tricky situation but we have lost our vision to see any way out. It's time to face up to your mistakes and move on with your life. Stop blaming other people for your mistakes. Learn to help yourselves and then other people will be more interested in helping you too. You do have the ability to get out of this mess.

212   Stop trying to save the world.

People can refer to you as having a kind heart, someone that cares for family and friends. You lend a helping hand whenever you are needed. While situations are running smoothly your efforts are well appreciated. As situations turn sour people look around to blame someone else. They will find it easier to blame you than to take responsibilities for their own actions. You will find yourself trapped in a battle to convince other people to see their situation from your perspective. In situations similar to this, take a step back from all the action and leave them to fight their own battles. You were doing them a favour so if they can't see that yet then it is their loss. Remember, you can't do everything.

213   Don't plant the seed of doubt.

When we observe a particular person, we may silently admire their appearance, yet when we look a little closer we can spot a blemish in their perfection. Rather than commenting on their beauty, we feel as though it is our duty to concentrate on their minuscule imperfections. That particular person may not had realised that their blemish was so noticeable and that single comment can change them from feeling confident about themselves to feeling insecure. They will not forget your comment and will have it in their mind where ever they go. Comment on people's efforts, courage and beauty rather than their inabilities. Plant the seed of success.

214   Learn to help yourself.

It's comforting to hear that we have compassion towards other people. We are greatly appreciated for our efforts towards helping other people in dealing with their issues. Our problem is that we can become entangled in other people's problems and neglect our own. Find time for yourself even if it means treating yourself every now and then.

215   How long can you think positively?

Plant a positive thought into your mind. Try to go into more detail. Multiply that thought. Think of a happy memory. Imagine how you will feel to finally succeed in achieving a long deserved goal. Concentrate on the steps that you will need to take in order to achieve them. Focus on a thought that encourages you to smile. Now plant another positive thought into your mind and go back through the other steps laid out. How long did you last before a negative thought popped into your mind? The more you practice this exercise, the longer you will be able to sustain positive thoughts. Train your mind to have the thoughts that will keep you thinking and acting more positively about life.

216   Force yourself.

There will come a point where you feel as though it's time to give up. You have tried your best but you still can't get past that particular hurdle. Your goal now seems out of reach and you can't see the point in pursuing it any further. The excitement that you once possessed has faded away and left you with an eerie feeling. It would be so easy to accept defeat at this stage as you are slowly running out of steam. Force yourself to complete tasks that are important to you. Divert your thoughts to ideas that will encourage you to pursue your goals once more.

217   Make someone's day.

Turning your attention onto other people should be getting easier as time goes on. You shouldn't feel as uncomfortable as you used to. There are a variety of ways to build people's self esteem. It could be a phonecall to say that you were thinking of them. You could give them a simple word of encouragement that helps to boost their confidence. Try taking someone out for lunch and offer to pay – for a change! You can visit a family member or even a dear friend. Offer your assistance when someone is least expecting it. Surprise someone by avoiding arguing in a particular situation. Get out of your comfort zone and try one of the positive phrases to help someone today.

218   Isn't life wonderful?

You are still experiencing problems although there are fewer due to you making better choices. There are still many outstanding goals and dreams to achieve, even though the increased level of confidence has helped you in achieving more than you would have previously. You still have room for improvement although your newly developed skills in dealing with people have assisted you in many situations. It all depends on which angle you are viewing life from but if you look carefully you will see that situations are improving because you are now able to deal with them more easily. The better choices you make in life, the happier you should feel.

219   You can't win everything.

Prior to all your races, you prepare yourself physically, mentally and even spiritually. Practicing everything needed to improve your skills to an unorthodox level. You have already won all the races in your country and you are now preparing for the Olympics. This is against other countries that have alternative training methods. Your race gets on the way and you feel as though you are off to a great start. As you rapidly pick up speed you quickly get into your correct form. You are ahead of everyone else and it also feels as though it could be your fastest time. Out of nowhere someone begins to overtake you. There is only a few seconds left to catch them but you already feel as though you are going as fast as you possibly can. Somehow you are able to pick up speed and you begin to catch them back up. Unfortunately you run out of time. You might have lost the race but you set a new record for yourself.

220   Be efficient.

When you purchase a new car you expect it to be reliable and not to breakdown every now and then. You may need it for a long journey so if you were aware that it has a history of intermittent problems, you would refrain from relying on that particular car. The more efficient you are, the more likely other people will be desperate for your advice and the quicker you will complete tasks.

221   You are not a loser.

The four hundred metre hurdle is one of the most feared races. It includes running and jumping over an extortionate amount of hurdles set at specific points of the track. Your first challenge is being able to jump the hurdles. Your next challenge is finding a smooth rhythm to be able to approach a hurdle without disrupting your pace. Most people would refrain from entering such a race because of the level of difficulty. Remember, you are a winner for just entering the race!

222   Monitor your tone of voice.

It can only take a slight readjustment of the tone of your voice to encourage people to listen to your advice. A small difference can change their perception of you from being aggressive to a sympathetic person. You can use the same phrase in different voices and it will create several meanings within their mind. Listen to your voice carefully and observe people's actions. You may think that you sounded fine until you see their reaction.

223   Know your competition.

You can avoid surprises by learning more about your competitors. There are usually other agencies that are moving similar products, especially in the corporate sector. Having more knowledge of their abilities and advertising campaigns will advise you on which direction to pursue and which ones to avoid. (Go to number 120)

224   Don't be ashamed of who you are.

When you have taken all the measures available to help yourself in looking more presentable, the rest is up to their discretion. Some people develop an inferior complex from being too self conscious of other people's perception of them. You are gorgeous but not everyone will have the wisdom to see that. Avoid focussing too much attention in trying to convince them that you are a trusted person. Be confident and find someone less judgemental.

225   Educate yourself.

It will help you on how to approach life with a more positive attitude. You will achieve more when you learn more about body language and human behaviourisms. The benefits of having a higher level of understanding can lead to you being more assertive, which will help you to land better leadership roles. Find out more about people skills, team work and other communication skills.

226   I'll be back.

Life has its ups and downs - similar to a roller coaster. One minute you are going up with the smell of success in sight, the next you are on your way down with the perception that you can't achieve any more out of life. Don't despair, help is on the way and before you know it, you'll be back on your way to the top. (Go to number 85)

227 Forgive but don't forget.

People can upset you which will cause you to replay a situation within your mind. Your thoughts will manifest to a degree that they become overpowering. Negative thoughts can drain you until you feel tired. Sometimes this can lead you to feel depressed over an issue that isn't even that important. Train your mind to let go of certain thoughts before you become physically, mentally and emotionally drained. Learn to forgive. Try to learn from every situation that you experience. Don't hold on to thoughts that can easily escalate out of control. Put them to the back of your mind so that you can finally move on.

228 Think of happy memories.

We all have cheerful moments in our lives that can uplift us in our times of despair. The memories can slowly fade away until there is little trace that they even existed. Brighten up your future by bringing these memories back to life. Share some of them with your family and friends and help restore a smile back to their miserable faces.

229 Choose wisely.

Some choices can easily be rectified when they result in an unexpected situation. While the result of other choices can cause a long chain of events, that can take years to correct. When you are faced with an important choice, take your time before deciding. Work out the consequences of each of your actions. Ask for assistance with your decision even if it involves phoning a friend. Use your option of fifty-fifty to reduce the amount of options left. Then delay while you workout the domino effects that will lead from each option, before you give your final answer.

230   Are you a quitter?

Learning to ride a bicycle starts off as an almost impossibility. Your parents remove the stabilisers and run alongside you until they feel as though you have enough balance to ride without assistance. They are wrong and you end up in a ditch – but you're not hurt! You brush off the dirt and get right back on your bicycle for another attempt. This time you fall off onto the grass – nasty parents! Do you quit? No; you get back on and keep trying – and your parents keep on running! Eventually you regain your balance and start riding solo. Your parents will agree that watching you ride for the first time is worth the long hours of running beside your bicycle. Next time you run into trouble and consider quitting, brush off the dirt and try again.

231   Spoil someone.

It should be someone that you care very much for. Maybe someone that is being neglected through no fault of their own, or a loved one who despite your odd working hours has always been there for you. It could also be one or more of your family members that deserves it because of their kind heart. It doesn't have to be something that involves a great deal of money. You could just spend a lot more time with that person and give them your undivided attention.

232   You can't do everything.

The more you seem to do, the more they expect from you. It starts off as an occasional offer but soon becomes a demanding chore. They seem to be calling on your assistance at every opportunity. Take some time out for yourself. Don't worry about them as though you are the only one available to help them. Share your responsibilities with others instead of overloading yourself with work.

233 Control your thoughts.

It's so easy to lose control and allow ourselves to be ruled by our thoughts. We have to first realise that we can control our thoughts to a certain degree in order to gain the ability to choose. Think of a cheerful memory. Now think of your favourite colour. You chose what to think of and you can do it more often when you begin to believe in yourself again. With more practice you will notice that you are no longer thinking and acting spontaneously. Regain your control before your destructive thoughts becomes out of control.

234 Desperate times calls for desperate measures.

When your back is against a wall, you will do almost anything to get away from your opponent. Sometimes we land ourselves in situations that we struggle to sort out on our own. We feel as though we have no choice but to ask for assistance from other people. It may have to be someone that we previously told we could manage without their help. Some people appreciate being needed and will be grateful to be of some assistance. Control your thoughts and avoid thinking too deeply into a previous issue, as it will prevent you from asking for help despite your desperation.

235 Don't assume the worst.

Some situations can appear to be worse than they really are due to the amount of time we dedicate to that particular issue. When we are in the wrong frame of mind to deal with issues we are already setting ourselves up for failure. We act according to our thoughts which mean us dealing with situations negatively because of our initial thoughts. Take more time to look at situations from a more positive angle and they will also turn out how you perceive then.

236   Physical conflict is a waste of flesh.

Some situations can become so heated that they end in physical violence. Most conflicts can be avoided when you approach them with the correct manner. If you feel as though a discussion is about to get out of hand, force yourself to walk away. It shows your high level of maturity to be able to walk away as it is much easier to use violence. Show them your ability to control situations by having a calmer voice which alone can defuse situations. Be aware of your body language and place your arms down by your side. Stay out of their comfort zone so as not to aggravate them. Always be on your guard just in case the discussion becomes more intense. As an adult, we need to show children correct morals on how to deal with heated situations.

237   I know that you can do it.

Show people that you believe in their ability to succeed. It can take just a few words of encouragement to catapult people's tolerance onto the next level. Help people to become more passionate about their goals. Encourage them to change the way that they think about themselves.

238   It's fine to feel nervous.

Some of the top boxers in the world enter the ring full of confidence and psyched up for action. Their eyes show you that they are focussed and ready for battle. Many of them will also admit that five minutes prior to entering the boxing ring, they were being sick due to nerves. The adrenaline rushing around their body prepares them to fight at the same time as making them feel ill. Once the fight begins, they are no longer nervous. You can adopt the same attitude by psyching yourself up to tackle the tasks that you are nervous about. (Go to number 14)

239   Time does heal.

Recent issues are fresh in our mind and can take up a large portion of our daily thoughts. We build on a few thoughts to draw up different conclusions of what could have happened if we had handled matters differently. After a short while we can multiply our thoughts to a degree where we have produced over a hundred different conclusions. As time goes on we experience more situations that become higher on our priority list. We slowly put our original issue to the back of our mind as we continue to find other more important issues to concentrate on. As more issues arise, our other thoughts fade away taking some of the pain and emotions attached to them away too.

240   We all have a story to tell.

You may learn about someone refusing to give up hope that has experienced numerous family problems that left them for dead. There is also a great deal for us to learn from hearing about your story. Writing some information about your life can be cathartic. You don't have to ever get it published. The simple task of writing down some notes can help to take a load off your mind. What's your story?

241   Learn to handle criticism.

There is a great deal to learn from receiving constructive criticism as it gives you guidance on improvements. Unfortunately, most criticisms are from people that don't particularly care about improving on your abilities. They comment on issues that they have little knowledge on but can cause maximum damage to some people's self esteem. We all have a few friends that act inappropriately and judge people at every chance they get. Be prepared to cope with comments that you won't particularly like or else one day they might catch you off guard and succeed in planting the seed of doubt. (Go to number 120)

242 Don't let people take advantage of you.

There are insensitive people that will take advantage of your good nature if you allow them to. They keep asking despite your efforts to hold your composure. They have a nasty habit of pressuring you in a manor that makes you feel uncomfortable or even guilty. Don't give in to their manipulation. If you give them an inch, they will take a mile. Learn to stand up for yourself.

243 Keep your opinions to yourself.

Most people don't value your opinion. It is far too easy to take them the wrong way and then cause more friction than solutions. Once the damage has been done it is almost impossible to correct. They will only remember their perception of what you were trying to achieve. We are all opinionated to a certain degree but we need to control what we say and sometimes bottle it up inside. It is not always better to speak your mind.

244 Turn a negative into a positive.

After encountering negativity we are left with the choice of accepting defeat or to move onto new pastures. As you change the way that you think about yourself, negative issues should become less affective. The bad news can toughen you up for your next encounter. Treat negative situations as learning experiences.

245 Discipline.

When we are studying for an exam and listening to music at the same time, it is very easy to get sidetracked as one of our favourite records begins to play. Although studying is our main priority, other issues can soon cloud our mind. Decide which one is more important at that moment and then force yourself to focus on that particular issue. Control your urges so as not to sway from important tasks.

246   Give people a chance.

People haven't acquired the same standard of wisdom that you have developed, but they are drinking from the same fountain of knowledge. They still haven't developed the thirst for success. Give it more time to take affect and soon they too will see the world as clearly as you.

247   It's what's inside that counts.

It's quite easy to tell someone that you care about them but you can find it difficult to show them. It can appear as though you are ignoring or mistreating them because they are drawing up the wrong conclusions. Some people are selfish or inconsiderate and it can be those factors that are preventing them from seeing the real you. As long as you meant well, give them a chance to look beneath your surface to see your true personality and if they can't, then move on.

248   Stop waiting in anticipation.

Are you still waiting for situations to improve? Most situations don't improve by themselves. They take a great deal of hard work. Most of our efforts are wasted as we have little to show but we need to be persistent. If you have a brick wall in the way of your success, turning your back on it will not make the wall disappear. When you decide to turn around you will see that the wall is still there waiting for you to deal with it. Don't expect other people to help you break it down until you start the quest yourself.

249   Face your fears.

We have already learnt that our fears are false, now we need to face them. Some of us are fearful of flying. We can almost have an anxiety attack everytime we think about it. The thought of being so high up or visualising the effects of the acceleration, can be overbearing. Once we have attempted it, our fear of flying will be slightly less traumatic. The more frequently we face our fears, the less anxious we will become.

250 Other people would swap their problems with yours.

When you buy a car, you expect it to run smoothly. It can create electronic problems that force you to book it into a garage. A few weeks later it is due for a service and you find yourself paying more money than you expected. You then get a puncture and have to replace a tyre in the rain. You complain to someone else about your problems and they inform you that they were not earning enough money to afford a car in the first instance. They would find it a privilege to own a car!

251 It's okay to have a moan.

Everyone has a little moan at some stage in their lives. Don't feel ashamed but also don't allow your moaning to get out of hand. After a while you will almost feel comfortable and before you realise it, you're moaning all the time. Take a short timeout and then divert your thoughts onto more positive issues.

252 You are not a robot.

How much can you take? People can share their distresses with you as though you are made of steel. They throw their problems at you without considering the effects that it's having on you. Although you may be perfectly capable of controlling your emotions, eventually you will become distressed too. Don't burden yourself with everyone else's problems. Leave some space to deal with your own.

253   Don't believe rumours.

People will do everything in their power to see you give up and fail. They will invent stories with the hope that it will intimidate you enough to surrender. You will feel so uncomfortable that you experience emotions that can lead to anger. Don't let the intimidation cloud your mind and break down your defences. Possessing a negative attitude is counter productive. It can affect your performance and you will soon lose your focus. Then it will prevent you from excelling to the next level. Redirect your thoughts onto your immediate issues – your goals.

254   It's never easy.

When you first started driving it felt as though you were a natural – well that's what you told people. You couldn't wait to be put in for your driving test. After overcoming your nerves you finally sit the test. You then find out that you have failed. Do you quit? You feel as though the roads were made for you to drive and so you retake the test. After you failed for the second time, you are once again faced with the same choice. This time you take more time before retaking the test. During that time you consider quitting on many occasions. Finally - after an emotional battle, you retake the test and pass on your third attempt. Success is never easy but well worth the struggle.

255   Have a good imagination.

Fashion designers have a great imagination. They have the ability to visualise designs in their mind before placing anything on their sketch pad. You can invent success stories within your mind as you grasp the ability to control your thoughts. Invent situations and visualise your ideal outcomes – it's fun.

256   It's not where you're from but where you're at.

There are certain issues in our lives that we cannot change. Where we were born and brought up was in other people's hands and we were too young to be able to choose for ourselves. Now that we have come of age, we can choose where to live. We can also change our careers starting off as a shop assistant and ending up as a top sales director. Some people have even started off at school as a destructive student that was expelled for hacking into the computer server, then ending up as a top computer analyst. We all have an issue that we would have preferred never took place. It's time to accept it so that you can move on with your life. He without sin, let him cast the first stone (John Chapter 8).

257   It's nice to be appreciated.

When you have helped other people in dealing with their issues, the feeling that you experience after they inform you of how much they appreciate your help is immeasurable. Your self confidence receives a well deserved boost and it uplifts your spirit. Some people can become so overwhelmed with emotion that it brings tears to their eyes. It also encourages you to go out and help someone else. Next time someone helps you, share your appreciation with them.

258   Where there's a will, there's a way.

High jump is your speciality. As the bar gets raised, you work extremely hard in finding ways to get over it. Your challenges get harder as the bar is raised once more. It doesn't matter how many times you jump over it, you don't seem to be able to clear it. The task appears to be impossible to complete. Then you conclude that you will approach the bar backwards instead of jumping it front facing. Your calculations are correct and you are able to clear the bar with ease. The bar is then raised to a ridiculous height that you fail to clear. After careful consideration, you realise that you will need assistance in reaching that height. You look around and see a long pole. Your high jump becomes pole vaulting as you use the pole to catapult you over the bar once more. Whenever you feel as though your options are exhausted, use your surroundings.

259   I did it.

Can you imagine the feelings of achieving yet another goal? Most of the time we concentrate on the principals in achieving a goal but sometimes we need to imagine that we have already succeeded. Placing yourself in this zone attaches more passion to your need to succeed. Another light will shine upon you revealing a new meaning to your situation. Use this quote aloud as though you have already achieved your goal.

260   I'm always right.

Create an attitude that builds up your self esteem. Approach people and answer them as though you are positively sure about the information you are sharing. Use your knowledge of body language together with good posture to help convince them. Help to change the way in which you think about yourself by pretending to be better than you are. Eventually you will become that person. You can have a more outgoing personality as long as you believe in your ability to change. Find other ways to boost your confidence.

261 Learn to sell yourself.

Have you noticed that some people appear to be able to sell almost anything? There is an art to being a successful sales person. When you observe their actions, you will notice that they possess the same qualities. They are extremely confident putting a great deal of enthusiasm into every word. Their posture and body language are present prior to their initial approach. People are drawn to them almost as though they are magnets. Once they have gained eye contact, it is maintained in a clever way that promotes trust. People then feel more comfortable sharing their views with them. They show great interest in what people are trying to obtain and possess the power of persuasion. Their suggestive manner creates a need for other people to want that particular product. Coupled with their non aggressive persistence, people are convinced to agree with them.

Don't take no for an answer. Be prepared to find another way of persuading them. Make it sound urgent as though it's the last one. Have the confidence to attach a time limit to slightly convince them to make a decision sooner rather than later. Approach each situation as though it's a game because they too may be trying to persuade you to give them the best deal. (Go to number 132)

262 Don't worry about bad minded people.

There are people that seem to be growing impatient, waiting for you to fail. Some people mostly speak about you in a negative way. They are in search of finding a way to get through your tough skin because they prefer you to stay on the same level as them. Keep focussing on your goals and take little notice of their intentions. Use their negative attitude as a positive compliment to your character. Put up your defences and don't allow them to break through your armour of steel.

263   Don't be greedy for success.

At lunchtime you are told to gather around a large table with other people. Then chop sticks are attached to your hands so as to prevent you from using your fingers. They are no ordinary pair of chop sticks as they are two metres in length. As you look around you notice that everyone is wearing them. A mountain of food is then placed in front of you all. It comprises of all your favourite dishes. Your tummy rumbles with hunger as it reminds you that you are starving. How will you manage to eat?

When you desire more out of life, be prepared to help other people first. The more you give, the more you will receive. Don't try and take everything for yourself. Feed other people and someone will feed you. When you are too greedy, everyone suffers.

264   Is it that important?

Is it worth the mental torture? Pursuing our goals and dreams can leave us feeling both mentally and physically drained. It can leave us so emotionally distraught that we are confused with which direction to pursue in next. Take a step back and have a moment or two to contemplate the real benefits. Then prepare a new strategy to help you back onto your journey towards enlightenment.

265 No pain, no gain.

Who said that it was going to be easy? When a boxer enters the boxing ring they are already aware that their opponent is out to hurt them. It is obvious that they want to cause them so much pain that eventually they will give up. In preparation for the contest they work extremely hard in toughening themselves up to be able to withstand an extortionate amount of pain. Their training includes finding out what their opponent is capable of and working out strategies to overcome them. They are well disciplined and focussed on their goals. As the match gets underway they both begin to experience numerous amounts of punches. Although there were many times of despair, one of their strategic methods pays off as they force their opponent to concede. The winner is ecstatic about their victory and bears the bruises to remind them of their struggle. Are you prepared to withstand an extortionate amount of pain in order to achieve your goals?

266 Have good public relation skills.

You need to be aware of the variety of people that you may come into contact with on your road towards success. The way in which you speak to your family and friends may need to be modified to help other people in relating to you. This doesn't mean a complete personality change as you will feel too uncomfortable. Some people are very intuitive and will be able to pick up on your discomfort. It may be a case of only making a few minor changes to feel as though you belong. When you are expected to speak in front of a crowd of people, use your knowledge of body language and communication skills to assist you. Speak clearly and try not to rush. Deliver your speech confidently and don't show fear. Have patience because with time comes experience and eventually you will no longer feel nervous. It's perfectly normal to imagine that there isn't an audience and that you are in a little bubble. Imagine that you are somewhere else that you would feel more comfortable. Don't forget to remind yourself to smile.

267 Customers prefer service to price.

Showing adequate customer service skills are of the utmost importance when in your place of work. Customers expect a high level of people skills. They will be looking for someone who is prepared to listen to their dissatisfactions and keep the debate non confrontational. You need to possess good communication skills and handle each situation with compassion. People expect each member of a customer service team to show a high level of understanding. It can only take one person to let down a team and change the attitude of the customer towards the whole team. Show them that you are not insensitive and that you respect their views. Agree with them whenever necessary. Apologise for any inconvenience caused and then offer them an alternative solution to their dispute. When you refrain from speaking your mind you will help them to feel more comfortable, which will inevitably lead to repeat business. Act positively on feedback and be prepared to compromise if an agreement can't be reached.

268 Have a positive attitude.

Remaining positive requires an unprecedented amount of determination. Most of the time, you will feel as though you are alone as the majority of people express a negative attitude. Maintain your composure and focus on your goals. The more positive attitude you portray, the less likely you will quit and the more chances of success. It takes a great deal of willpower and strength to have a positive attitude towards the challenges of life.

269   Negative thoughts lead to negative actions.

Have you noticed that whenever we feel as though an idea will fail, it does? Our thoughts lead us to a chain of actions. If we think something is doomed to failure then we act in a negative way which eventually leads us to failure. We need to break out of our usual routine and think more positively despite whether a situation ends positively. Changing our routine thoughts will increase the chances of success. Negative thoughts bread negativity.

270   Let it go.

There are situations that become worse with the more effort we put in. The more we chase the further it seems to run. We become emotionally attached and find it difficult to accept that it is doomed for failure. People keep all kinds of birds as pets. They train them, feed them and look after them as though they are one of the family. Whenever they let the birds go, they have a choice whether to fly away to freedom or to come back to a happy home where they are fed and looked after well. Deal with your situations in a similar fashion. If it's yours then let it go and it will come back.

271   Life is an endurance test.

The ultimate prize is £10,000. The test includes running six miles in under thirty minutes, then watching the shopping channel for three days without sleep and without the use of a toilet. You will then have to crawl through a long, dark, muddy tunnel infested with cockroaches and other creepy crawlies. Then walk barefoot in a room littered with spiders, to reach and eat food with your dirty, muddy fingers. Would you do it? We all have different amounts of challenges that we can endure before we finally give in. Prepare yourself for your next test. (Go to number 194)

272   Be suggestive.

Can I make a suggestion? Try it for a while and see if you have a higher success rate! Develop ways to encourage them to follow your advice. Find and act on their weaknesses. Use your strengths to your advantage. Ask questions and be a good listener. Be persuasive and use your communication skills. Don't be too quick to admit defeat. Try it for a while.

273   Fight for what you want.

How would you feel if you lost it forever? There are certain things in life that are not worth battling over as we can live quite comfortable without them. There are also things that we have become so immensely passionate about that they have become a necessity. If it's that important to you, put your boxing gloves on, get in the boxing ring and let the battle begin.

274   There's no 'I' in team.

Each person involved in a customer service team represents the whole team. They should all show honesty and integrity at the same time as having proficient knowledge of their products. Each person needs training on communication skills and customer service care. When a situation arises each person should portray a high standard of customer service care. It only takes one person to let down a team so each decision should be made as a team.

275   Don't overload with negative information.

Our brain holds negative information similarly to a pressure cooker. The more we hear, the hotter it becomes until it begins to incinerate our positive thoughts. The pressure cooker temperature keeps rising in accordance with the amount of heat it receives. As more of the water turns to steam, the pressure builds up. It is at this stage when an outlet needs to be created to let off steam before the pressure exceeds the maximum capacity and blows the lid off the pressure cooker. When the pressure in our minds exceeds the amount that we are capable of taking, it overloads capacitors and resistors and slowly corrodes our mind. The corrosion then allows depression to infect our electrical circuit. Create an outlet and protect your mind before the pressure builds to a level that causes damage. Find a way to let off steam before it's too late, even if you have to take it all out on a punch bag.

276   Be compassionate.

When you take time to observe other people you will notice that some of them need more help than others. Observing other people will help to speed up your reaction to know when people are in need of your assistance. Be prepared to move out of people's way when you feel as though they will struggle more with manoeuvring around you. Show other people that you are thoughtful and not insensitive. Have patience when listening to other people. It shows that you are a caring person.

277   Think more highly of yourself.

There are ways of breaking out of our routine thoughts about ourselves. Some of us are extremely self conscious. It's difficult for us to think of a single positive word to say. We need to find ways to build up our confidence even if we start of pretending. It is possible to turn around our negative thoughts to a more positive approach by adding a little humour. Create a habit and imagine that people are looking at you because they think that you are gorgeous and irresistible to look at – I hope that made you smile. Imagine that the people you just passed are turning around to take a second look at you. Tell yourself that you are sexy and smell gorgeous. There are other ways to encourage yourself to smile and feel better of yourself. Why don't you think of a few?

278   People want you to get ahead but not ahead of them.

Some people are very selfish and don't realise how hard we have been trying to improve our lives. They haven't got the slightest idea of the amount of sacrifices we have made. They constantly think of cunning ways to hold us back. Sometimes they even pretend to be proud of our achievements but on the insides they are routing for our failure. Don't allow their views and opinions to hold you back. Reinforce your iron armour so as not to let anything they say or do get through to you.

279   Are you content with what you have?

If you are happy with what you have already achieved, then anything more is a well deserved bonus. We can become too engrossed with achieving our goals and become greedy. There is no harm in striving for more as it gives us something positive to concentrate on. Working towards some goals can be seen as therapeutic as long as you refrain from taking them too seriously. They can open up new doors of opportunity and the benefits will be rewarding. It really does pay to keep going. There is nothing wrong with wanting more but don't expect it.

280 Another round.

When we are up against a worthy opponent in a boxing ring, we need to be prepared for a tough fight. As the contest starts we throw punches from every direction but they all fail to make an impact. Our opponent then delivers a few punches at us which seem to hit us hard. We then throw a shower of punches towards them but to no avail. After successfully dodging some of their attempts, somehow one gets through to us and it knocks us to the canvas. The effects of the punch are extremely painful as we land on our face. We are down but not out. The thoughts rush through our mind as we contemplate whether to admit defeat. As we are slowly counted out, we take timeout to regain composure. Once we have gathered enough strength, we get back to our feet before we are counted out. The contest restarts and we attack at a greater speed. A few of our punches get through as they begin to back off. They return harder than before and we are forced into a corner. There we trade punches pound for pound in hope that the other person becomes exhausted. The bell sounds to signal the end of the first round. As we sit there gathering our strength, we also attempt to work out another plan of attack. The bell sounds once more to signal the start of round two. It can take several rounds before you finally work out a strategy to overcome them. Don't throw the towel in yet. Take some timeout to gather up more strength. Be prepared for a tough fight.

281 Be helpful.

Look carefully and you will see that some people are in need of more help and assistance than they request. Some of your family and friends are either shy or feel embarrassed having to ask. Be more observant and offer your assistance. At this stage you should be thinking of other people more regularly. Try not to feel confined to only be thoughtful once a month. Help people if and when needed but also be cautious so as not to be taken advantage of.

282 Don't appear to be desperate.

Chasing too hard after some of our goals can sometimes appear as though we are desperate. We might have a target to reach within a certain period of time and need to encourage a few more people to agree. Our presentation can slightly dwindle as we grow more eager. The pressure to deliver can sometimes lead us to almost force people to conform.

Maintain your composure and give people a few options. Try not to appear as though you are not busy by running through a long list of dates where you are available. Be assertive and confident as though you are busy but that you are prepared to fit them in to your schedule. Prepare a few phrases in advanced to appear sophisticated and organised. Find out why they will be better off accepting your offer and gently persuade them by making them feel as though it's almost a necessity. Be compassionate and inform them that you will appreciate their support immensely. Be also prepared to continue at a later date and then try to find someone else that is more willing to agree.

283 Be a good loser.

Many successful people will admit that on the way to success they suffered a few failed attempts. They had times where a sure winner ended unsuccessfully. Rather than becoming bitter and blaming other people for their mistakes, they have stood up and admitted to being at fault. Learn to control your emotions so as not to get carried away with rage. Use it as a way of toughening you up for your next challenge. Walk like a champion and keep searching for that business venture that will proclaim you a winner. Learn from the situation and let it encourage you to be more determined. Don't take it to heart as you have to lose sometimes to give other people a chance.

284   Less haste, more speed.

Getting something done quickly isn't always the best way to get the job done. Performing tasks at high speed increases the chances of making mistakes. When we have gone over a task to find and correct the problems, we end up spending more time than we would have if we had taken our time in the first instance. Dealing with situations cautiously leaves less room for unnecessary mistakes. Sometimes performing tasks at a slower speed results in them being done more proficiently and efficiently.

285   Control your actions.

There are people that still are not convinced that we can control our thoughts but there is a substantial amount of evidence to prove that we can control our actions. It's so easy to get ourselves into trouble and then suffer the consequences of our actions. We need to learn how to control how we react in various situations. This can be achieved by retraining our brains. Exercise your mind by practicing a few simple exercises. Next time you have an itch, refuse to scratch it for at least ten seconds. When your phone next rings, delay answering it for a few seconds while you compile a few rehearsed responses. When you next get the urge to go to the toilet, choose to wait another five minutes – but don't make a mess! If you suffer from obsessive compulsive disorder (OCD) and you repeatedly wash your hands, control your ritual once a day. If you have a phobia of spiders, next time you see one don't scream, just run! You are in control of your thoughts and actions. It's only a matter of time before you realise it too.

286   Other people are worse off.

Other people would love to have half the amount of confidence that you possess. They admire your qualities and would appreciate being able to have the strength and courage to pursue their goals as you do. People want your charm, your wit and will power so that they are able to deal with the challenges they are experiencing. Keep your eyes focussed on your goals and pay less attention to your problems.

287 Learn to trust someone.

We have worked extremely hard to get where we are in life. Our business is running pretty smoothly but only because of the amount of time and effort that we have dedicated. Although it would be great to take some time off and get away for a few days, we feel as though we are married to our job. The thought of trusting other people to run our organisation while we are away scares us. If you are becoming increasingly tired from performing a multitude of demanding tasks, then it's time to find someone else that's trust worthy. Offload some of your work load and stress and delegate responsibilities to a colleague that you have trained to take over when you are away. You can't do everything on your own and you need time to yourself or time with your family.

288 Beauty is in the eye of the beholder.

At our first glance someone will look beautiful yet other people fail to agree with us. Also there are people that we perceive as average but after we get to know them we feel as though their beauty has suddenly become radiant. We all have different perceptions of beauty. If you truly think that something is beautiful, then it is.

289   Respect your parents.

There are too many people these days that disrespect their parents. It's usually because of a trivial issue that has been blown out of proportion. This is a direct result of a negative thought that has escalated out of control. Calm down and tackle the issue rationally. Sit down and work out what your parents have done for you. Perfect parents don't exist so they can't do everything right. They are allowed to make mistakes too. If you took some time to write things down, you would realise that they do plenty for you. Money doesn't grow on trees so you shouldn't expect to receive everything that you ask for. A good parent shows you love and affection which is more important than the money. Good parents don't need to earn respect because they brought you up and looked after you for many years. That alone deserves respect. Try not to be so bitter because your parents won't be around forever. If the day ever came when you lost them, you would eventually realise that you were taking them for granted. Then you may become depressed with guilt as your conscience eats away at you. Learn to stand on your own two feet and don't keep relying on them for everything. Cherish the moments you have with your parents and stop wasting precious time.

290   Speak positively to yourself.

Thinking of positive thoughts encourages you to be more productive. You have been taught a variety of quotes and phrases that will enhance your self esteem. It is recommended that you verbally communicate them as well as just thinking of them within your mind. It makes each phrase more powerful when you speak them out aloud. You are a winner, you can do it and you are gorgeous; now practice saying them regularly.

291   Say 'thank you' to people.

We all know how to say 'thank you', so why don't we use it more regularly? I was always taught: If you know something but you don't follow it, then you don't really know it. If we know that it's good to have manners then we should practice it. Learn to say 'thank you' more frequently because it is better to use it too often than not often enough. Manners don't cost anything but can make someone's day.

292   Use reverse psychology to get your own way.

When women cry, men melt and then bow down on their knees. They are not really upset, they are merely playing a game and trying to see if they can connect with your emotions. The more emotional they can make you, the more they can get you to agree on. You can use it to your advantage too. Act grumpy and they will think that you are hungry. Then they will feed you in hope of cheering you up! It also works when you are trying to get someone to agree with you. Instead of constantly chasing, tell them to forget it because you didn't think that they would agree anyway. Some of us like to prove people wrong.

293   Be grateful for what you have.

It is important to have a positive attitude towards life, even when situations don't work out according to plan. We can easily become too disappointed from not achieving some of our goals. When we take a step back and look at our achievements, we will notice that we have achieved an ample amount of success. Don't be too greedy. Life isn't about how much money you can make. It's about being happy with yourself.

294   Be strong.

You will encounter challenges that will almost push you to your limit. During the earlier stages you have been taught many coping techniques. Now it's time to put them all into place to build up your armour of steel. You are capable of handling the pressures of life. Never give up; don't give in; you're going to make it. Be persistent and believe in yourself and your abilities. Show people that you have built up your self confidence to a level that can cope with an incredible amount of stress. Prepare yourself for the battle ahead.

295   Find more ways to encourage a smile.

Many of us walk around with miserable faces because we are too busy thinking of our challenges. The more negative we feel, the more negativity we tend to spread. Learn to contain your problems while you are in the company of other people. Try not to infest them or you may accidentally divert them from pursuing a goal. Look for ways to encourage people and not discourage them. Work on your posture so as to rub off your positive attitude onto other people. Think of words and sentences that bring a smile to your face. I'm sure that you can think of some people's names to make you smile. Help other people to follow your example and smile more when in public. Don't forget to deal with your problems when you get home.

296 Learn the importance of good money management.

There are people that have spent most of their lives building up a successful business. They succeed in creating a handsome income that many people would envy. Instead of putting away some of their income for a rainy day, they decided to squander their wealth. After a while of enjoying themselves, the market changed and it forced them to close. Unfortunately they didn't have enough income put away and they had to declare bankruptcy. Learn control and show people that you have good wisdom. Enjoy your money and your life but also put away a certain percentage in a secure bank account. Some businesses can disappear quicker than it took them to be created. Nothing lasts forever. Be wise and save for the future.

297 You are allowed bad days.

On our way towards success we overcome many hurdles. We encounter huge challenges and somehow work out ways to conquer them. Several more awkward problems are placed before us to test our staying power. They nearly drive us to our breaking point by draining away all the positive energy from within us. After fighting against all odds we are able to emerge triumphant.

Then along comes a small, insignificant problem, a problem that on a good day would have been referred to as trivial. It seems to push us overboard and we become emotionally distraught. We breakdown and even begin to cry. Try to give yourself some time to recuperate your strength. Find something that makes you want to live again. Once you are revitalised and feel strong enough, you will be able to tackle such problems with ease. There are always going to be obstacles in your life so find more ways to withstand the pressure.

298   The glass is half full.

There are two completely different ways of viewing a glass. When it is half filled with wine, many people will perceive it to be quite a lot and be satisfied with their measure. While there are a few people that really enjoy their drink and will expect an undeserved top up because they feel as though their glass is half empty. One group is completely satisfied with their drink while another group of people are utterly dissatisfied to the point where they complain. The group of people that felt that it was half full are all happy with life but the others are disgusted with their rationed portion. The different ways in which we view our lives makes a huge difference to our attitude towards life. Be careful with which one you choose.

299   Actions speak louder than words.

We visualise ideas within our mind. Some of them sound promising so we even share them with other people. They advise us to expand on our thoughts and to put them down on paper. Although our life would be drastically improved, we never get around to doing anything about it. Talk is cheap. Don't allow your dreams to fade away. Act on them instead of verbally expressing them on a regular basis. We all have the potential to live a more comfortable lifestyle but it's up to you to do something about them. It's time for action.

300   Re-train your mind.

Our brain can be compared to a computer. It processes a mass amount of information and is expected to deal with it all at high speed. Under normal circumstances it works very efficiently and programs load up quickly. When it encounters a serious problem and is infected by a virus, it has to perform a list of troubleshooting tasks. Some viruses are persistent and attach themselves to secure files so that they cannot be erased. This then causes serious interruptions to software programs. Using a virus protector will eliminate most of them but there are a few viruses that spread quickly and cause mass destruction. When you load up software programs, they either take longer to load or they fail to load at all. The longer it takes for us to correct the fault, the more files that become corrupted. The damage can become permanent and you will be left with no choice but to wipe the hard drive and reinstall all your software programs again. Some computers are more susceptible to viruses and it is recommended that they have a reliable virus protector. We are used to a certain routine, a way in which we process our thoughts. Sometimes our mind becomes infected with viruses and it is necessary to retrain our mind to process thoughts efficiently again. Install your virus protector to eradicate negative thoughts.

301   Boost people's confidence.

Help to build up people's confidence so that they believe in themselves more. Tell them good things about themselves. Inform them that some other people were speaking very highly of them. Let them know that you thought that they handled a situation brilliantly. Inform them that you enjoy watching how they deal with difficult situations because you learn a great deal from them. Watch how they grow in confidence.

302   Think ahead.

It can be related to that of running towards a corner. You are concentrating on gathering speed to approach it as fast as possible. As you approach at high speed, you prepare to shift your weight onto your outer foot. This will help you to veer off in another direction with the minimum delay. Once you reach the corner, you start to shift your weight. Just at that moment someone appears from the corner but is running towards you. You were not expecting it and you collide into them with great force. You now suffer the pain of failing to take other circumstances into consideration. Take into account the consequences of your chosen actions. Avoid unnecessary surprises and visualise what obstacles might be around the corner.

303   Rule your destiny.

Some of us dislike the job that we have chosen. We frown at the thought of returning on a Monday morning. In our spare time we dream of what life would be like if we changed our career. Although it's a small step in the right direction to dream, it's even better to take action. If you are no longer happy with your chosen career, take the steps needed to change your future. It is also some people's life long desire to be free but they are not ambitious enough to start their own business and follow their dreams through to the end. Most of us want more out of life but only a few of us are prepared to do something about it. Don't retreat, don't surrender. Have the willpower to pursue your goals or you may as well put up with the stresses at work. Until we can do things for ourselves, we must do as we are told.

304   Stop making sense of nonsense.

A friend of yours failed to ring you for a few weeks. They usually ring on a regular basis but the phonecalls seemed to stop after an intense discussion. You remembered having a dispute about the way you handled a particular situation. A thought or two flashed through your mind reminding you of some of your comments. Then a web of thoughts escalated and you soon realise that they are annoyed with you. When you thought about it further you work out that they were the ignorant one and if they are playing a game, then you won't have any of it. Now you become distraught and decide not to contact them either. This goes on for a few more days and the more you thought about the original issue, the more conclusions you draw up that always fell in your favour.

Then an early phonecall to you gives you a surprise. It is your friend calling to apologise because they forgot to pay their phone bill and were temporary disconnected. They apologised immensely. After asking them if they were upset with their previous discussion with you, they informed you that they realised that your views of the situation was correct and that they understood how you felt. You on the other hand, had built up an imaginary situation that now seemed very real. They never had any dispute with you in the first instance, yet you wasted vital brain space in search for an answer that would explain their lack of communication.

305   Be proud.

You are an inspiration to other people. Your positive attitude has helped other people to see a brighter side to life. There are plenty more people to motivate and encourage. People rely on your strengths to restore belief in themselves. Be proud of what you have achieved.

306 Recognition – children cry for it, men die for it.

How does it feel to be rewarded for your efforts? A football team can struggle to win a few games but when they find out that they have done enough to make it to the top of the league, their attitude soon changes. It drives them harder to achieve more. Winning something boosts your confidence level. Now they try extra hard to remain at the top for the rest of the season. It also feels good to know other people recognise your abilities. Continue working hard at achieving your goals and sooner or later people will show their appreciation and select you for an award.

307 Time is money.

Sometimes our search for perfection can lead us to waste valuable time. Many people are paid by the hourly rate and will benefit from our lack of organisation. If you are losing money because your staff appear to be procrastinating, find someone else to get the job done faster. Be a leader and make an important decision, whether to encourage them to finish the task quicker or to pass the responsibilities onto someone else.

308 Always be on your guard.

You can avoid being surprised by running through a list of possible scenarios and planning your choice of action. Imagine what could happen after you have made a decision and then visualise different outcomes. Be ready for anything, including other go-getters. You may come across someone that possesses your qualities and skills. They will have the power of persuasion and will try to catch you off guard. It may feel as though you have to agree with their proposal because they are trained to sound convincing. Never underestimate your opponent and refuse to sign until you have taken a day or so to think it through. Always prepare for the unexpected.

309   We will all encounter stress.

During our lives we will encounter problems that will leave us feeling stressed. How we handle the stress will depend on how tough we have become. As we grow older, our health will slowly deteriorate. Some of our friends and family will become seriously ill or even pass away. Other people we know may suffer from a traumatic episode that leaves them feeling depressed. On top of all that we will have ourselves to worry about. We may be experiencing one or two health issues at the same time as fighting against the obstacles put before us that are trying to prevent us from achieving a goal. The weaker we are, the quicker we would already be feeling stressed. The stronger we are, the more stress we can withstand.

There are ways to toughen you up to withstand the pain. Having a positive attitude towards life; avoiding negative influences and realising that your problems are trivial compared to others, are some main principals in becoming more resilient. When you have become exhausted with the pressures of life, you are more susceptible to stress so find something that helps to lift up your spirit. Exercise reduces stress hormones so enrol at your local gym. Keep your hopes up or else you are sure to feel down. People are relying on your strength to uplift them. You have the power to strengthen the weak.

310   It's not over until it's finished.

During a game of battle ships, we suffer a few moments of despair as we consider quitting. Our opponent has successfully sunk most of our ships and we have yet to find one of theirs. Another hit sinks another one of our ships as we become distressed. The game goes on and we are now down to our last ship. We decide that it is a silly game and contemplate surrendering but we are persuaded to see it through to the end. After a short while we finally search out a ship and succeed in sinking it. They struggle to find our last ship while we begin to sink their ships one by one. The game grows in intensity as we become more excited. Another few missiles hit their ships and they seem to be sinking more rapidly. We become nervous as we slowly work out their strategy and find where they hid the mass portion of their fleet. All we have to do now is survive and completely sink all of their ships before they search out and find the last of ours. They fire a missile and miss our ship but they are now convinced of where we are positioned. We have no choice but to make a successful strike or we would surely lose. After carefully selecting a position, we fire our last missile. It's a hit and we succeed in sinking their last ship. We jump with excitement as we celebrate our victory and the end of an enjoyable game! Don't give up until it's completely finished.

311   Draw up a business plan.

What do you want to achieve? Work out some short term and long term goals. Find out what you would like to achieve within twelve months and in the next two to five years. Formulate strategies to guide you on your journey. Try to think step by step rather than focussing too far ahead, as it may give you a daunting feeling. You will be then put off because you have very little to show for your loyal efforts. Set mini goals and daily tasks to encourage productivity. Try your hardest at achieving your goals and be persistent. Organise brain storming sessions with colleagues to create a multitude of ideas to work on. Don't be too proud to seek advice from a reliable source. Use other people's experience (OPE) to broaden your knowledge or to refer to when giving people advice. Ask customers for their views on your customer service. You can also learn from their feedback for future improvements. Take time to rearrange your products to make them look more appealing. Learn from observing your competitors and act accordingly. Have a game plan and several backup plans to make sure that your business is running efficiently. (Go to number 122)

312   Any publicity is good publicity.

Several companies purposely have negative advertising campaigns to create gossip. Using the power of word of mouth, their ideas quickly spread. They can sometimes shock the general public but at the same time it is spreading their company name. They will time it right and publicly apologise for the misunderstanding. They will then explain their business plan which will include their persuasive tactics that will create a need for people to purchase their product. Most people will then see the positive side to their campaign and will be well aware of their product. It's risky, but it works. It may be necessary for you to hire someone else to handle advertising tactics. Advertising in local newspapers or on radio stations, is a common way to get publicity. Seek ways to let your advert stand out from the others. If most adverts are light, then produce a dark advert. Most adverts are now dark so either have a light one or go for colour. When people first see your advert, they need to read the most important section first. Enlarge these sections to create interest. Many people read the right hand pages automatically. Use this information to either place your advert there or to create a spectacular advert on the left that is eye catching. Leaflet drops are a good way of testing out new ideas. Try different things but most importantly, have patience. Rome wasn't built in a day.

313   What you don't know can't hurt you.

You visit your local superstore to purchase a small bag of potatoes. When you return home you place them straight in your oven because you are starving with hunger. Then you prepare a salad with your usual variety. Still feeling peckish, you help yourself to a few – four, scones. The scones tasted delicious, so good that you were tempted to eat the rest. They filled the gap and kept you going until the jacket potatoes were ready.

Then a friend visits – they must have smelt the food, and you invite them to have a jacket potato with you. Your friend eagerly accepts your invitation and hovers around your kitchen in anticipation – greedy! While you are preparing the food, you ask them to help themselves to the last two scones. They hastily agreed and removed them both from the packet. Within seconds they devoured the scones and enjoyed them immensely. They enjoyed them so much that they asked you if they can have another one. You reply to them that they were the last two but then they informed you that there are two more in the cupboard. When you looked, you saw the two scones that you had left. Then you realised that you had bought another packet two weeks previously. You then discreetly read the use by date on both packets. It revealed that the scones in your packet were still fresh but the scones that your greedy friend ate were not! You both sat down and enjoyed your jacket potatoes and you kept your little secret to yourself.

314   Have courage.

The greatest show of courage was from Nelson Mandela. He fought for the rights of his country, trying to bring peace back into the world. He battled against all odds and was sometimes alone on his quest for peace. The world wasn't ready for his views and he was placed in prison. During that time he wasn't disheartened and found other ways of being heard. He was locked up from 1964 – 1990 when he was finally released. During that time he remembered his purpose and never lost sight of his goal. For twenty-seven years he refused to give up hope and had the courage to pursue his mission to the end. In 1994 he became the president of his country. Are you prepared to wait twenty-seven years to achieve your ultimate goal?

315 We are not all equal.

We can sometimes be quite ignorant to what is really happening around the world. It's common sense to assume we are born with two arms and legs. If we are asked how many fingers are on a human hand, then our answer is always five. Yet when we take a closer look at each other, we will discover the real picture. Some people are born with six fingers and others are missing limbs. We are not all born with the ability to hear, see and speak. There are even disabled people without the sense of touch. Does a deaf and dumb person have the same potential to achieve things as we do? The reality is very scary and almost unnerving. We all have slightly different potentials. Are you living yours to the fullest?

316 It is better to have won and lost, than never won at all.

During the course of our lives, we strive to achieve a multitude of goals and dreams. Some we reach and others we don't. There are also those that we gain and then lose further on in our lives. Although it is a very painful experience to lose something so precious that you have worked extremely hard for, at least you have had a taste of success. Some people spend their whole lives chasing dreams that they will never reach. They suffer years of heartache and pain. Enjoy your moments of success because it can be taken away from you at any time.

317 Sometimes you have to be cruel to be kind.

Placing a metal shoe on a horses hoof can look cruel and painful. Hammering big nails into the bottom of their feet is almost unimaginable. Yet if they didn't have them, their feet would become more damaged. This would eventually cause more pain and suffering. Sometimes you have to refuse to perform certain tasks as it would have led to them taking advantage of your good nature. People need to realise that they can't have everything they ask for. They need to try harder at doing things for themselves. It will also teach them the importance of good money management. Teach people good morals even if you appear to be slightly cruel.

318   Don't bite the hand that feeds you.

We can have a few family and friends that we lean on for support. They help us out when we need someone to share our issues with. They even take time out to listen sympathetically to our problems. We can then turn selfish and show our ignorance towards them by not being there for them whenever they are in need of support. Appreciate other people's kindness and be prepared to return the favour. When people realise that you are an attention seeker and show little emotions towards their troubles, they will no longer be interested in supporting you in your time of need. Don't be selfish, be kind.

319   Have peace of mind.

The way in which we deal with individual situations can leave us wondering whether we handled them correctly. It starts off with us helping and assisting people as much as possible but then someone plants that nasty seed of doubt into our mind. This then leads to us questioning our own actions.

Other people can sometimes expect too much from you and you can find yourself trying to stretch further than you can reach. As long as you know the truth in your heart and really feel as though you have done enough, that's all that matters. Don't allow them to make you feel guilty. Do good and good will come back to you.

320   Delayed gratification.

Reaping the rewards of our work can sometimes take years. There is often a long, almost quiet patch where we feel as though nothing is going well. During these moments it would be extremely easy to throw in the towel and quit. It's when we have had enough of trying so hard without seeing the benefits of our struggles. When things are going well, we are all full of confidence and advice. It's when things are going wrong when our true strengths are put to the test. Learn to have a little more patience. Instead of waiting to the end of the month to be paid, you have to wait a few years but don't worry, you will be paid and given a handsome bonus for your loyal efforts.

321   It's all experience.

Why are we encountering so many challenges? Every obstacle placed before us is there for a specific reason. They are there to help us become tougher so we are able to withstand other challenges. Once we have overcome an obstacle, others of an equivalent size or smaller, are like a walk in the park – easy. We then see most challenges as trivial. Our experience also reinforces our strength so we have a greater chance of overcoming larger challenges. There is something to learn from everything we see, hear, think and do. There will always be obstacles and we have the choice of whether to give up or deal with them face to face. Treat it all as a learning curve.

322   Be a great friend.

There are friends that we consider as almost acquaintances due to the infrequency of their contact. We all need help and assistance at times and it's a comforting feeling to know that we have a friend that we can rely on. When your friend is in need of emotional support, don't be just a friend, be a great friend. Contact them regularly, even on a daily basis when they are feeling extremely low. Your sympathetic support will help to prevent them from becoming depressed. Some friendships are more important than materialistic achievements.

323 Don't count your chickens before they hatch.

There are people that are prepared to undo what you have worked hard in achieving. While you are celebrating the possibilities of your success, other people are seeking ways of preventing your achievement. Avoid exposing yourself to cunning plans. Be on your guard at all times. Don't assume success until you are grasping it firmly in your hand as there are no guarantees in life.

324 Keep your chin up.

There will always be other chances to succeed, even though we feel as though we have lost everything. When we become exhausted from our efforts, the easiest option is to quit.

It's a rough ride and only the strong survive. Hold your head up high and keep trying. Focus on your goals and don't become sidetracked with alternative thoughts that will lead you to failure. Be proud of what you have achieved. Never give up on your dreams. Success can either make you or break you.

325 When the going gets rough, the tough get going.

Life is a test that we are supposed to be tough enough to complete. We need to build up our wall of defence until it is as big as a mountain. The pressures of life will come and slowly wear down our wall until it begins to crumble. When our wall is replaced by a mountain, the same pressures of life make a lesser impact on our exterior. This is why some people seem to be less affected by pressure. Seek alternative ways to build up your wall of defence until it is as tough as a mountain. Then you will be able to withstand much more stress than the average person. Be as solid as a rock to avoid being knocked down.

326   Be fearless.

The story of David and Goliath shows the ultimate example of bravery. He was of a mediocre size and faces Goliath - a giant. David had to plan his line of attack in great detail before attempting to accomplish such a mammoth task. After running through all his possibilities, he came to the conclusion that he would surely be defeated in an unarmed battle. Rather than admit defeat, he chose to use a sling shot to overthrow his huge opposition. After catapulting a rock, Goliath was eventually knocked to the ground from which he never rose. Be prepared to try almost anything. Show your confidence in dealing with awkward situations. Get out of your comfort zone. Control your emotions and refuse to allow the size of challenges to put you off.

327   Be considerate.

Take other people's feelings into consideration. They might have a disability and need help and assistance. Try not to assume that they will ask as they sometimes feel as though they are a burden on other people which will deter them from asking for help. Be prepared to put other people first. Learn to apologise for any misunderstandings, even when there is a chance that you were not at fault. Avoid arguments whenever possible.

328   The only way is up.

After a long struggle, we can sink to the bottom. An unexpected chain of events has left us in an emotional state that seems endless. The psychological consequences leave us struggling to function normally.

Take responsibility for your actions and regain control over your life. You are already at the bottom so you can't go any lower. Every positive action you make will be a step up in the right direction. Even if you are broke to a degree of bankruptcy, you can recover. Curb your spending and transform yourself back into a respectable human being. Learn from your mistakes and take measures to become more resilient in stressful situations.

329   Be prepared to walk the walk.

There are people that sound like experts when giving advice on what to do in certain situations. They are quick to voice their opinions on matters that they have yet to encounter. They express their feelings with great passion as though they are prepared to lead by example. When they are eventually faced with a similar situation, they act in a completely different manner. Back up your words with action. Demonstrate your confidence to follow through. Show other people that you can do more than just talk the talk.

330   Finish what you started.

Achieving goals can take longer than we first anticipated. Other issues can be an additional input to us becoming less interested. Studying at college is one of the most common goals to be affected. Courses usually run for a year. After a few months we get sidetracked and then boredom sets in. Before we realise it, we have lost the passion to continue.

Redirect your thoughts to your initial reason for starting on your quest. Search deep to find other factors that will refuel your passion. Once you are mentally ready, don't lose sight of your goals again.

331   Seek and you shall find.

Stop rushing around sporadically. Organise your search carefully and diplomatically. Be totally committed to your ideas. Look around and observe your surroundings. There is usually a small, blurred sign that is slightly out of your focus but it contains important facts. The information you require is hidden within its contents. Make it your mission to achieve it before the end of the year. Continue on your quest despite any obstacles you encounter. Listen to other people because there is a great deal to learn from them. Their speech might spark off an idea that catapults you dangerously close to your goal. Be patient and the answers will come to you.

332   It's not just what you know, it's who you know.

Knowledge is a key factor in producing success. Its ingredient prepares you with the necessary materials to refer to when needed. Most challenges can be eliminated using the self help techniques. Many of your obstacles can be overcome when you have help and assistance. Knowing the right people can also help to avoid a series of difficult situations. Making fewer mistakes also helps in speeding up the process of success. Utilise every opportunity to increase your chances of success.

333   Look to the future.

We tend to live in the past, replaying situations within our mind in hope of receiving a satisfactory explanation. Unfortunately they are rarely acceptable and we are drawn back to that moment in time. After a while we can find ourselves repeating an incident similarly to a scratched record.

Accept the past so that you can finally move on. Turn over to a new chapter in your life. Your future is in need of some delicate attention since it has been neglected for a good period of time. Make preparations for more important issues and avoid concentrating on previous events. You can't change the past but you can set your future.

334   I am successful.

Your training is almost complete. Each exercise has been carefully selected to represent a particular quality that you will need to possess. They build up your confidence and prepare you to face difficult tasks solo. Success is not an easy road so you will need all the help and support available. The advice will enhance your abilities and toughen you up for any challenge. Repeating this phrase will boost your self belief and put you in a positive frame of mind. Prepare yourself for a rough journey. When trouble comes knocking at your door, be ready.

335 Never give up hope.

Waiting for situations to materialise can be related to that of hanging on a rope. Our problem is that we can't visualise that we are about to be rescued. The signs are unclear and we are becoming increasingly tired. Holding onto the rope is pushing our abilities to the limit. The temptation of releasing our grip is almost as great as the rewards.

Don't allow the conflicting thoughts to get the better of you. There is too much to lose from letting go. It's too far to fall after all the effort you have devoted with the hope of succeeding. Give it a little more time to work. Hold on tight to your dreams. Never let go because help is on the way.

336 Agree to disagree.

Some people have a warped point of view and will not be able to see things from your perspective. You are pretty convinced that you have the solution but proving it is turning out to be quite a task. Persuading other people is taking up too much of your valuable time and beginning to stress you out. Why argue? It's clear that they are not going to agree with your proposal so try to think of an alternative plan. When an agreement can't be reached, sometimes agree to disagree and then move on to the next issue.

337 Broaden your horizon.

Tunnel vision can affect more of us mentally than being physically visually impaired. The inability to see the benefits of our actions will prevent us from achieving more. Obstacles are put in our way to discourage us and lead us to believe that we are incapable of succeeding.

If you keep telling yourself that you are nothing then you will amount to nothing. Enjoy your life to its fullest. Readjust the way that you think. Try to see life from other people's perspectives and open up new doors of opportunity. There is usually more than one way to reach goals so be prepared to consider other options. Some work quicker and other routes can take longer but they both eventually lead to your ultimate goal. Have a more diverse approach to your tasks and get more out of your life.

338 Businesses encounter low points.

There are patches where businesses don't profit as well as other times. There is always a quiet period before a storm. Everywhere will seem calm even though there is a vast amount of activity going on behind closed doors. We can't visualise it yet but people are discussing our business opportunity. The silence can discourage us from pursuing ideas positively. Then it can drive us to believe we are useless and never really had a chance of success.

Have a plan of action that keeps you busy during the quiet period. Soon it will pass and you will be rushing around frantically, trying to keep up with the high demand.

339 Think of positive phrases.

It can be used as a distraction to redirect your thoughts onto a positive subject. They also teach you principles of how to deal with the variety of situations. There are many more than are listed and we all have a few personal ones that are close to our heart. Use them wisely to direct you on your journey or you may find yourself floating around like a piece of paper in the wind.

340 Moan for fun!

Learning to control our thoughts enables us to manage problems more effectively. Our new found strength also gives other people the opportunity to take advantage and moan more frequently. Some of them have good cause to complain, while others centre on minute problems that will be eradicated on a single command. Making better choices is all it takes to cure many problems. When someone frequently complains of a trivial problem, redirect the attention back onto you and have some fun. Share a small issue with them and observe the cunning ways in which they try to continue spreading their dissatisfactions. Don't look for any sympathy as they are more interested in wallowing in their own self pity. Remember to be there for anyone who sincerely requires your help and advice.

341 Love one another.

Hatred carries its own seed of destruction. Its existence breeds negativity which spreads quicker than a virus. The seed grows until it infects other parts of our body. Our trust in other people is broken down as we gradually become more ill. It changes our attitude towards life and eventually we stop caring about anything positive. The hope of achieving our goals and dreams is consumed with bitterness.

Restore your faith in other people. Learn how to trust people by controlling your paranoia. Let go of your hatred and bitter feelings and allow love back into your heart. The happier you feel, the easier you will find it to deal with challenges. Love conquers all.

342   Be prepared to make sacrifices.

Problems are there to discourage us from going any further. We encounter some challenges that require us to work extra hard. This involves juggling two or three jobs at the same time or working extra hours in our present job. It won't leave us much time for ourselves or other people that mean a great deal to us. Although it is a temporary situation, it can last quite a long time. Many people want more out of life but are not prepared to make the necessary sacrifices in order to succeed. Have a plan of action that will show you the best route to take. (Go to number 129)

343   Don't procrastinate.

At any given time, we are working on several issues simultaneously. The ones that are at the top of our list of priorities can take its toll and wear us down. It is far too easy to put them on hold and decide to leave them until later. After just a short while we can become busy with other tasks and lower them in our list of priorities. Learn to recognise the signs to avoid wasting valuable time. Ask yourself how important each task is to you. Be prepared to divert your attention from the less important issues. Continue on your quest for completion. (Go to number 19)

344   Stand up for yourself.

Bullies come in all shapes and sizes. They can appear in schools, colleges and our workplace. Many of them are big, bold and ugly, putting us on the spot for an immediate reaction. The worst ones are those that take a more subtle approach. Most of the time we don't even realise that we are being bullied. They slowly chip away at our self esteem, breaking our defences down until we lose the strength to fight. They can start off as friends or even bosses, ordering us around a little more each day. Part of their mission is to see how much they can get away with.

Don't tolerate this behaviour any longer. Be more assertive and don't let people push you around. They will manipulate you into thinking that it is part of your job to assist them but really they are cleverly playing with words. Inform other people of your dissatisfactions. Share responsibilities where ever possible. People will take advantage of your good nature as long as you allow them to.

345   A problem shared is a problem halved.

Are your problems becoming too big to handle? Dealing with problems alone can drain us to the point of exhaustion. The lack of strength leads us to believe that we have reached a dead end with no way out.

Sometimes just talking about your unsolved issues helps to alleviate enough pressure to be able to see another way out. Contact a sympathetic friend and share some of your issues without expecting them to give an opinion. The less anxious you feel, the more problems you will be able to withstand.

346   Different strokes for different folks.

When several people are given the same task to complete, they handle them differently. Several people feel as though their world is falling apart. They seem to almost crack up under the pressure. While other people tackle the situation more diplomatically. They then announce that it wasn't much of a challenge. Be prepared to take alternative routes to avoid unnecessary obstacles. Deal with each challenge calmly, as though you know that you will eventually succeed. Some of us hope that the stress and worries will disappear by themselves but they don't, so learn to deal with them.

347   If you know why, the how will come.

Ask yourself, why do you want it? Our goals can sometimes feel slightly out of reach. We know what we want but we are not sure exactly how to attain them. This is usually because our goals are not important enough to us. Place your goals into your imagination. Dream-build, to allow them to seem more clear. Picture yourself in hypothetical situations, touching, seeing and enjoying your achievements.

Make your goals even more important to you. Become highly passionate towards them. Visualise the reasons why you need them so badly. Make an informed decision to pursue them to the end. The extra effort that you devote into achieving them will give you an uplifting feeling. Now that you are excited about them, your mind will start to work wonders. Without realising it, your mind will automatically search for ways of how to reach them. In just a short moment you will be another step closer to your destiny.

348   Knock and the door will be opened.

After a while, we can become tired of chasing our goals and dreams. The high volume of rejections leads us to believe that we were not cut out to succeed. Some people even try to discourage us with their negative opinions. Every door of opportunity we try seems to be locked and now we are feeling weary.

Keep the pressure up. Be persistent because one of the doors will turn out to be your access to success. Once you find it, other people will admit that they knew that you would reach your goal. Your knuckles will become sore from the vast amount of doors that you knock but you have to be determined to find the one that will be opened for you. When you feel too burdened with trouble and pain, ring the bell. Keep progressing until you finally succeed. (Go to number 26)

349   Stay around positive people.

Have you noticed that when someone yawns, you are tempted to yawn too? That's because yawning is contagious! Seeing someone else performing this act triggers off a chain of thoughts in your mind, which leads you to feel as though you should copy. This is why it is advised to stay clear of negative people. Although you may feel as though you have a strong personality, eventually you will be tempted to follow suit. You too will develop a distorted view of life. Negative people don't care whether you succeed or not. They are oblivious to the amount of good people that they infect.

Positive people show empathy towards your feelings and will offer their assistance wherever possible. Mingle with them and their positive influence will soon rub off onto you. The positive influence will springboard you up to another level, a level which will be much closer to your goal. You are what your friends are so stay around people that will point you in the right direction.

350 Motivate other people.

We know what we need to be doing to travel on the shortest road to success but we can become distracted by the numerous activities happening around us at any given moment. When we hear the same advice from other people, it sounds much more interesting and it then inspires us to do whatever it takes in order to move on. Other people also need you to motivate them. Show them how to deliver themselves correctly to avoid unnecessary obstacles. Help them excel to the next level so that you can all prosper together. A few words of wisdom is all it takes. Be a motivator. (Go to number 56)

351 Have a great personality.

Some people have a nasty habit of prejudging other people before even meeting them. Instead of giving people a chance to prove that they have a warm personality, they judge on their own previous experiences. Their words can be powerful enough to put us off someone. That behaviour is frowned upon and we should avoid people with those characteristics. Rise above them and get to know people first. We should be prepared to give people the benefit of the doubt and allow them to impress us. Greet people with a warm smile and try to get to know more about them. Be the one to promote conversation. Show off your communication skills. Find something, like a certain outfit, that makes you feel more confident. Make sure that your personality is so appealing that people remember you. Be a people person.

352   Lead by example.

Do you want to live at the mercy of other people? When leaders quit, we consider quitting too. They are people that have inspired us, people that have helped us through our turmoil. They are people that we look up to and follow.

Unfortunately, everyone has their own set of problems and reasons to quit. It doesn't mean that you should give up on your goals just because they have chosen to stop pursuing theirs. Show them how it's done. Keep your eyes on your goals. Visualise their future potential to enhance their importance. Plan out some strategies in order to reach them. Networking your business idea at corporate gatherings should be taken into consideration. Have a well prepared presentation ready to deliver on demand and be prepared to go it alone. Follow your dreams through to the end. (Go to number 1)

353   Success is sweet.

Can you almost taste it? When crowds of people are running away from success, turning the other way you are sure to be knocked around, but it will be worth it. The thought of achieving your goals will help numb the pain. Show your dedication to your goals. Be determined to force your way through the crowds to the end. As you grow increasingly closer, you will become more excited and become eager to succeed. Money also inflates your ego and gives you that extra drive needed to get you through the final mass. Once you have reached your success, you will feel ecstatic. The pain and suffering that you experienced on the way will soon be forgotten. You will hardly be able to contain your feelings. Your emotions will run high and you may even cry, but with sheer excitement. Keep working hard. Success is just around the corner.

354   Be proactive.

Dare you pursue your conquest to the end? We can all become busy chasing our goals for a while but only a few of us possess the staying power. It feels as though we are chasing one dead end after another but there is a way out.

Find ways to keep yourself active. Search every inch of your mind for the answers. Experience teaches knowledge. Learn from every situation that you encounter until you find the way out. Continue to keep busy and be almost in a hurry, as you can't enjoy the beauties as much when you become older. Your journey is nearly over. You are going to make it some day. You are going to be somebody.

355   Do a good deed.

Have you ever helped a stranger? Offering our assistance to other people should almost be second nature. Develop a craving to help people. It can be friends, family or even strangers. Maybe it is someone that is at the cashier's desk in front of you and is struggling to find some loose change to pay for their shopping. Or maybe you could give some money to a homeless person. Just hearing someone say 'thank you' or 'God bless you' should be satisfying enough to you. Do good and good will come back to you.

356   Read motivational books.

Reading helps to override our negative thoughts. It teaches us how to develop the main criteria necessary to withstand the stresses of life. We will all encounter challenges during different stages of our lives. The challenges are much easier to deal with when we possess a higher level of positive understanding. The information fuels our mind and prepares us for action. It takes one month for our mind to fully digest the information. Then we need to read another book to refuel once more. The longer we are without the correct influence, the hungrier we become. When we are too hungry, we begin to feed off alternative fuel supplies. That gives negative thoughts a chance to multiply. Every thought has a meaning, every action has a purpose. Block out negative thoughts before they grow out of control or else they will drive you to do something that you will later regret. Read a book to build up your confidence and heighten your self esteem. Refuel your mind today.

357   Ask and it shall be given unto you.

We often assume that people will not be interested in our business ideas. Sometimes we avoid them and end up approaching someone else. The person that we thought would be more interested turns us down. Then to our surprise, the person that we first anticipated wouldn't be interested, shows interest. They even ask us why we failed to approach them sooner.

You'll never know unless you ask. Don't be shy and miss out on important opportunities. Dismiss the negative thoughts. There are people out there that are in need. Sieve through the time wasters and you will find the go-getters.

358   Be teachable.

It feels uncomfortable having someone else correct us, especially when we were so sure that we were handling matters adequately. When we take a serious look at our circumstances in question, we will notice that things are not running perfectly. That means that there is room for improvement. Other people might possess the information that we need.

Be prepared to try something new. Listen intently to the advice that you are being given. After you have taken it all in, choose the components that you would like to put into action. Don't be stubborn and return to your old habits. You don't know everything. There is always something to learn from every situation.

359   Open your eyes.

Many of us are surrounded with so much bitterness and rage that our personalities are affected. The kindness within us is buried beneath a mountain of anger caused from a direct result of encountering too many challenges. Don't despair, help is already here. People are helping you out of tricky situations yet you fail to see. Many of the problems that you are complaining of are no longer there. Open your eyes a little wider and you will see that you haven't got anything to worry about because you are no longer alone.

360   Show affection.

Some of our lives are filled with so much heartache and pain that we slowly transform into a robot. We turn off our emotions so as not to be hurt anymore. It is our way of dealing with the problems that we are experiencing. Suppressing our feelings is an easy way of dealing with challenges but deep down, we are still not quite happy. Learn to embrace your problems. Don't leave them unsolved, deal with them. Once bitten, twice shy. Face up to your challenges and avoid making the same mistake again. Move on with your life. Express your emotions. Give someone a hug! Share your heart with someone more deserving.

361 Men cry too.

When we advise other people that it's perfectly normal to express your emotions, we are disassociating ourselves. As an adolescent, we are told that men don't cry. It is drummed into us for many years until we finally believe it. We are led to believe that showing our emotions makes us appear less of a man, yet when we fail to show our emotions, we are told that we are cold hearted. We can't win!

You can't stop people from having their own views. When a situation arises that drives you to the point where you feel emotional, let it out. You will feel much better expressing it rather than suppressing your feelings. Men cry in secret anyway or after their favourite football team loses! We all have emotions so don't be ashamed of yours.

362 I refuse to lose.

Our destiny has not yet been written. This means that we don't know what will happen in the end. It also means that we have control over what happens... now.

Rule your destiny. Choose your path wisely. Set yourself goals and then work extremely hard in order to attain them. Don't accept failure. There will be huge challenges to overcome on the way but as long as you have faith in your abilities, you will eventually succeed. Don't lose sight of your goals. Be determined to see them through to the end. Make a decision to fight for them despite the temptations to quit. This is a race that you have entered to win.

363   Good always triumphs over evil.

How can one person be experiencing so many problems? Every day we face different trials and tribulations. Many of them test us to the limit and others push us way beyond our limit. Everytime we make a decision to tackle them with a positive attitude, another problem arises. It's almost as though there is an additional force acting against us, something that is determined to see that we fail. Our patience has been tested so many times, that it feels as though we have become psychologically scarred from the numerous attempts to succeed.

There is only a certain level of stress that we are able to tolerate before we begin to lose our patience. Learn some more survival tactics. Heighten your tolerance level so that it is harder for things to get to you. Keep your mind busy finding solutions instead of concentrating on the actual problem. Every day is a battle that you will overcome. Step by step you are getting stronger. Eventually you will overcome the enemy.

364   The road to success is not straight.

There is a curve called failure; a loop called confusion; speed bumps called friends and red lights called enemies. There are caution signs called family and flat tyres called jacks. But if you have a spare tyre called determination and an engine called perseverance; with insurance called faith and a drive to make it, you will eventually reach a place called success.

365 Life is the greatest gift.

What's the point in having lots of money when you can't enjoy it? Our bodies are put under immense stress to see how much it can withstand. The obstacles, challenges and problems manifest spontaneously as though they have a life of their own. Their uneven rhythm confuses our every thought. We call upon other people to help us overcome them but are far too often let down. Sometimes we even wish that we had never met them. An inkling leads to disaster, a positive action directs us to another dead end. Family question our motives and lend us little support. Friends try to discourage us but somehow find time to take advantage of our kind nature. When we have been put down enough times, eventually we believe it. We are now lost, with nowhere to go.

Our body is just a vehicle transporting our soul, it's what's inside that counts. Be careful what you wish for. Don't take anything or anyone for granted. As quick as you have them, they can be taken away. Don't worry about what other people think. All the pain and suffering that you have incurred has been for a good reason, to make you stronger and to know right from wrong. When situations don't materialise according to plan, be thankful for just being here as your life could have turned out much worse. Find your inner truths. Concentrate on the happier parts of your life and keep spreading your positive vibes all over the world. Don't lose hope when unsolved issues plague your mind. You have come across many dead ends throughout your life and you have been taught how to find another route out.

The journey to success is tough so you have to be tougher. There are no guarantees but you stand a much greater chance by merely entering the race. Next time you are feeling down, get up, stand up and don't give up the fight. Find and fulfil your destiny.

About the Author

Vendon Wright was born on the sixth of August 1966, in a small town called Rugby, in England. He was registered blind at the age of twenty-eight, after a ten year battle. He suffers from Retinitis Pigmentosa - RP, a rare eye disorder that slowly destroys the pigment cells in the eyes. So far there are no known cures. Battling against such a crippling disease led him through a labyrinth of challenges. His fight to remain positive was put under more pressure when he found out that he was also suffering from Ushers syndrome, a disorder that results with him going both deaf and blind.

His journey involved experiencing a wide range of emotions which was necessary in order of dealing with his disability. The issues and challenges became so intense that it brought him to a cross road where he had the choice to give up fighting against such a crippling medical condition or to continue on his struggles. It was at this point where he became a Christian and now believes that God is with him through all his struggles. After a long hard battle of overcoming huge obstacles, he finally learnt to embrace his medical condition.

Quick reference

1   Have goals and dreams to work towards.
2   Think positive not negative.
3   If I think I can, I can.
4   I'll feel better tomorrow.
5   I'm not scared.
6   Think of happy thoughts.
7   Good things come to those who wait.
8   Some will, some won't.
9   Everyone has problems.
10   Don't let anyone tell you that you can't.
11   Dream build.
12   Fear is false.
13   Enjoy your life.
14   I'm a winner.
15   Be a great listener.
16   Appreciate what you can do.
17   Everyone has choices.
18   When you're feeling down, go up.
19   Make a decision.
20   Never, never give up.
21   Workers are achievers.
22   Life is tremendous.
23   I haven't got any problems.
24   Smile.
25   I feel great.
26   Next.
27   Think big.
28   Have fun.
29   Go for it.

30   Be an encourager.

31   It's okay to cry.

32   Leaders lead.

33   I feel wonderful.

34   Stop moaning.

35   I'm gorgeous.

36   I am blessed.

37   You can do it.

38   It will be worth it.

39   Write things down.

40   Do the things people won't do, to have what they can't have.

41   Treat yourself.

42   Believe in yourself.

43   Read happy stories.

44   Have good people skills.

45   Learn to handle rejection.

46   I'm confident.

47   Stop waiting until tomorrow.

48   Don't cry over spilt milk.

49   You never know what you had until you lose it.

50   I deserve success.

51   Think of something funny.

52   Don't hold a grudge.

53   It's not over yet.

54   Calm down.

55   I am ambitious.

56   I believe in you.

57   You only have one life.

58   Don't worry, be happy.

59   Create a habit.

60   It's never too late.

61   I'm assertive.

62   If it's to be, it's up to me.

63   Be passionate.

64   Try, try and try again.

65   If the dream is big enough the facts don't count.

66   Yes I can.

67   I enjoy a challenge.

68   Music makes me happy.

69   I have the ability to succeed.

70   Think, before you act.

71   Speculate to accumulate.

72   You can't be up all the time.

73   Be thankful for what you have.

74   I feel lucky.

75   Strive for perfection.

76   Be nice to people on the way up, you may need them
      on the way down.

77   Practice what you preach.

78   Observe people's body language.

79   Be enthusiastic.

80   You're allowed to make mistakes.

81   I'm not shy.

82   Always look on the bright side of life.

83   The hardest step is the first one.

84   Be prepared to compromise.

85   Have faith.

86   Timeout.

87   Compliment someone.

88   Drown out negative thoughts.

89   Try another approach.

90   Greet people with a smile.

91   You are better than you think.

92   Life is one big road with lots of signs.

93   I'm a go-getter.

94   Everything will work out in the end.

95   They are making a big mistake.

96   There's a light at the end of the tunnel.

97   Patience is a virtue.

98   Have a laugh.

99   Have good posture.

100 Always give a 100%.

101 Surprise a friend.

102 Appreciate what you can see.

103 If they can do it, I can do it.

104 What's your dream?

105 Stop wishing.

106 Control.

107 It's okay to be scared.

108 You're a winner.

109 They are jealous.

110 I will find time.

111 Courtesy.

112 There are certain things that are out of our control.

113 Be consistent and persistent.

114 Don't make a mountain out of a mole hill.

115 Lack of confidence leads to failure.

116 Knowledge is power.

117 Yin Yang.

118 Life isn't fair.

119 Time waits for nobody.

120 Be prepared.

121 You never know until you try.

122 Learn to be more organised.

123 Duplicate yourself.

124 I am what I think I am.

125 Multiply a happy thought.

126 Spare a thought for others.

127 I agree.

128 Positive thoughts lead to positive actions.

129 Is it worth fighting for?

130 It's not what you say but what's in your heart that matters.

131 Keep your mind busy.

132 Know your product.

133 If you want positive advice, ask a positive person.

134 If you can't hear, you must feel.

135 Don't dwell.

136 It's acceptable to feel like quitting.

137 Negative eats away at us like a virus.

138 Enhance your memory.

139 Tell jokes.

140 Be sympathetic.

141 On the way to success there's always someone trying to put you off.

142 Motivate yourself.

143 External motivation.

144 Be aware of your surroundings.

145 It's a sin to waste a good talent.

146 Don't jump to conclusions.

147 We all have a point in which we can't go beyond.

148 There is only a thin line between success and failure.

149 Use your common sense.

150 Count to five before you answer.

151 Don't let people walk all over you.

152 Phone a friend.

153 Businesses are built on thin threads.

154 Use incentives.

155 Trust your instincts.

156 Perseverance.

157 Things can only get better.

158 Do you really want it?

159 Be friendly.

160 Just do it.

161 Everyone makes mistakes.

162 Learn how to meditate.

163 Learn to say NO.

164 Enjoy the chase.

165 Take care of your health.

166 Reap what you sew.

167 When it rains it pours.

168 Give constructive criticism.

169 I will always be there for you.

170 Look in the mirror.

171 Forget the past.

172 Don't put all your eggs in one basket.

173 Focus.

174 You can lead a horse to water but you can't force it to drink from it.

175 One step at a time.

176 Nobody's perfect.

177 Things could be worse.

178 Limit your negative input.

179 Be a peace maker.

180 Be hungry for success.

181 Work on your communication skills.

182 Have a positive attitude on the phone.

183 Be approachable.

184 Take no notice of gossip.

185 O.P.E – other peoples experience.

186 Treat someone else.

187 Don't let your mind drift.

188 Don't ask negative people for advice.

189 Be excited.

190 Team work.

191 End everyday happy.

192 Take risks.

193 Everyone has emotions.

194 Learn to enjoy a challenge.

195 Venture out of your comfort zone.

196 Stay out of other people's comfort zone.

197 Try to maintain eye contact.

198 Don't judge a book by its cover.

199 Learn from your mistakes.

200 Think yourself to sleep.

201 My problems are trivial.

202 Praise people for their efforts.

203 Make time.

204 Good things come to those who wait, but they come faster to those who work for them.

205 There are lots of signs in life.

206 Are you going to let someone put you off?

207 You can't kid a kidder.

208 Be determined.

209 Practice.

210 Verbal conflict is a waste of words.

211 Fix up.

212 Stop trying to save the world.

213 Don't plant the seed of doubt.

214 Learn to help yourself.

215 How long can you think positively?

216 Force yourself.

217 Make someone's day.

218 Isn't life wonderful?

219 You can't win everything.

220 Be efficient.

221 You are not a loser.

222 Monitor your tone of voice.

223 Know your competition.

224 Don't be ashamed of who you are.

225 Educate yourself.

226 I'll be back.

227 Forgive but don't forget.

228 Think of happy memories.

229 Choose wisely.

230 Are you a quitter?

231 Spoil someone.

232 You can't do everything.

233 Control your thoughts.

234 Desperate times calls for desperate measures.

235 Don't assume the worst.

236 Physical conflict is a waste of flesh.

237 I know that you can do it.

238 It's fine to feel nervous.

239 Time does heel.

240 We all have a story to tell.

241 Learn to handle criticism.

242 Don't let people take advantage of you.

243 Keep your opinions to yourself.

244 Turn a negative into a positive.

245 Discipline.

246 Give people a chance.

247 It's what's inside that counts.

248 Stop waiting in anticipation.

249 Face your fears.

250 Other people would swap their problems with yours.

251 It's okay to have a moan.

252 You are not a robot.

253 Don't believe rumours.

254 It's never easy.

255 Have a good imagination.

256 It's not where you're from but where you're at.

257 It's nice to be appreciated.

258 Where there's a will, there's a way.

259 I did it.

260 I'm always right.

261 Learn to sell yourself.

262 Don't worry about bad minded people.

263 Don't be greedy for success.

264 Is it that important?

265 No pain, no gain.

266 Have good public relation skills.

267 Customers prefer service to price.

268 Have a positive attitude.

269 Negative thoughts leads to negative actions.

270 Let it go.

271 Life is an endurance test.

272 Be suggestive.

273 Fight for what you want.

274 There's no 'I' in team.

275 Don't overload with negative information.

276 Be compassionate.

277 Think more highly of yourself.

278 People want you to get ahead but not ahead of them.

279 Are you content with what you have?

280 Another round.

281 Be helpful.

282 Don't appear to be desperate.

283 Be a good loser.

284 Less haste, more speed.

285 Control your actions.

286 Other people are worse off.

287 Learn to trust someone.

288 Beauty is in the eye of the beholder.

289 Respect your parents.

290 Speak positively to yourself.

291 Say 'Thank you' to people.

292 Use reverse psychology to get your own way.

293 Be grateful for what you have.

294 Be strong.

295 Find more ways to encourage a smile.

296 Learn the importance of good money management.

297 You are allowed bad days.

298 The glass is half full.

299 Action speaks louder than words.

300 Re-train your mind.

301 Boost people's confidence.

302 Think ahead.

303 Rule your destiny.

304 Stop making sense of nonsense.

305 Be proud.

306 Recognition – children cry for it, men die for it.

307 Time is money.

308 Always be on your guard.

309 We will all encounter stress.

310 It's not over until it's finished.

311 Draw up a business plan.

312 Any publicity is good publicity.

313 What you don't know can't hurt you.

314 Have courage.

315 We are not all equal.

316 It is better to have won and lost, than never won at all.

317 Sometimes you have to be cruel to be kind.

318 Don't bite the hand that feeds you.

319 Have peace of mind.

320 Delayed gratification.

321 It's all experience.

322 Be a great friend.

323 Don't count your chickens before they hatch.

324 Keep your chin up.

325 When the going gets rough, the tough get going.

326 Be fearless.

327 Be considerate.

328 The only way is up.

329 Be prepared to walk the walk.

330 Finish what you started.

331 Seek and you shall find.

332 It's not just what you know, it's who you know.

333 Look to the future.

334   I am successful.

335   Never give up hope.

336   Agree to disagree.

337   Broaden your horizon.

338   There are patches where businesses don't profit as well as other times.

339   Think of positive phrases.

340   Moan for fun!

341   Love one another.

342   Be prepared to make sacrifices.

343   Don't procrastinate.

344   Stand up for yourself.

345   A problem shared is a problem halved.

346   Different strokes for different folks.

347   If you know why, the how will come.

348   Knock and the door will be opened.

349   Stay around positive people.

350   Motivate other people.

351   Have a great personality.

352   Lead by example.

353   Success is sweet.

354   Be proactive.

355   Do a good deed.

356   Read motivational books.

357   Ask and it shall be given unto you.

358   Be teachable.

359   Open your eyes.

360   Show affection.

361   Men cry too.

362   I refuse to lose.

363   Good always triumphs over evil.

364   The road to success is not straight.

365   Life is the greatest gift.

Other books available

I was blind but now I can see

Through my eyes

About the book

During the course of our lives we encounter numerous obstacles that challenge us on every level. They vary from stressful situations to issues concerning our perception of ourselves. Some of the challenges put us under such immense pressure that there are days where we feel as though we could do with a little help and support. Since our daily problems change, it is also necessary to have a variety of techniques to suit.

One a day addresses the main principals of living a happier life, in greater detail. It covers techniques on confidence building, communication skills, how to deal with stress, handling rejection and dealing with criticism. Using the step by step guide increases our tolerance level to stress and restores our belief in our abilities. There will be days where we need tips on self help and other days where we require advice on becoming more successful.

One a day has an inspirational phrase for every day of the year. Train your mind to divert your thoughts as you rapidly grow in strength. Read one a day and watch your personality change for the better at the same time as becoming more confident and successful.

Lightning Source UK Ltd.
Milton Keynes UK
UKOW04f0857150715

255211UK00001B/14/P